CULTURE MEETS POWER

Stanley R. Barrett

Westport, Connecticut
London

Library of Congress Cataloging-in-Publication Data

Barrett, Stanley R.
    Culture meets power / Stanley R. Barrett.
        p. cm.
    Includes bibliographical references and index.
    ISBN 0-275-97807-9 (alk. paper)—ISBN 0-275-97808-7 (pbk. : alk. paper)
    1. Power (Social sciences) 2. Culture. I. Title.
HM1256 .B27   2002
303.3—dc21   2002066340

British Library Cataloguing in Publication Data is available.

Library of Congress Catalog Card Number: 2002066340
ISBN: 0-275-97807-9
        0-275-97808-7 (pbk.)

First published in 2002

Praeger Publishers, 88 Post Road West, Westport, CT 06881
An imprint of Greenwood Publishing Group, Inc.
www.praeger.com

Printed in the United States of America

The paper used in this book complies with the
Permanent Paper Standard issued by the National
Information Standards Organization (Z39.48-1984).

10 9 8 7 6 5 4 3 2 1

Dedicated to the memory of two irreplaceable brothers and two dear friends.

Thomas Barrett
Graeme Barrett
William Graf
Do Quang Kim

Contents

Preface

This is a good time to be an anthropologist. From theoretical to applied work, the discipline is flourishing. Doubts about whether we could survive in a post-colonial world have been laid to rest. Indeed, anthropology has emerged as a leader in the investigation of the forces of globalization. Nowhere is this more evident than in the recent attention given to power. Armed with concepts such as hegemony, discourse, and resistance, anthropology has reinvented itself as the study of power, in the process partly turning its back on culture.

I began this book with the intention of evaluating this new love affair with power, including how power had figured in the discipline in the past, and whether the affair was destined to be a long-term one or an intense but brief embrace. While power remains my main focus, what I soon discovered was that I could not avoid culture. To a very large extent, the rise of the concept of power and the decline of the concept of culture are one and the same process.

Not all anthropologists, incidentally, have been pleased that power, at the expense of culture, has taken the discipline by storm; nor is there universal agreement that power is a negative, destructive force, or any less ambiguous than other concepts such as culture or community. What is clear is that with rare exception in the recent literature, whenever culture has met power, culture has been the first to blink.

Many of the most insightful comments about power are found in philosophy, political science, and political sociology, and I do not hesitate to raid from them whenever I see an opportunity. Throughout the study I have tried to ground my arguments in ethnographic data and real-life situations; it was with this in mind that I decided to add a postscript about the terrorist attack of September 11, 2001, on the World Trade Center and the Pentagon, the circumstances of which go to the core of this study.

Some of the ideas for this book, particularly those concerned with power and racism, were tried out at the University of Memphis in January, 2000. I am grateful to Professor Tom Collins for inviting me to participate in the Charles H. and Phoebe McNutt Advancement in Anthropology Lecture Series, which that year celebrated the work of Professor Eric Wolf. I also wish to thank Professor Andra Thakur and Dr. David Thomas, Vice-President Academic, for inviting me to talk about power, culture, and globalization in a public lecture sponsored by Malaspina University College in Nanaimo, British Columbia, during the fall of 2001. Colleagues and students too numerous to mention have influenced the direction of this study, but I would be remiss if I did not mention John McMurtry, the late Bill Graf, Sean Stokholm, Sean Norton, Jeanette Burke, Georgia Marman, Elaine Bauer, and Sean Hier. Ed Hedican and Neil MacKinnon early on encouraged me to tackle the topic of power, and Michel Verdon wisely counselled me on an especially sensitive section of the study. With her usual grace, efficiency and eye for clarity, Kaye prepared the final typed version of the manuscript. Finally, I owe a great deal to Jane Garry, the ideal editor, whose support, sensitivity, and wisdom were simply inspiring.

Most of this book was written during the winters of 2000 and 2001 in a little hotel in Portugal, where I probably was the only guest not displeased when it rained. My thanks to Mr. Hernani Correia and his exceptionally considerate staff for making my visits to Portugal so pleasant. I am grateful to administrators at the University of Guelph for permitting me to arrange my teaching schedule so I could write in such a conducive environment. Somehow I forgot to make it clear that one of the metaphorical messages in this study is that some people in power, including the odd administrator, should be skinned alive.

Chapter 1

Why Power?

Why has power recently captivated the anthropological imagination? Perhaps the answer is no more complicated than the fact that it permeates our daily lives and intrigues us, for reasons cynical or otherwise. But surely that's nothing new. Maybe we have finally embraced Leach's assertion (1954) that it is power that drives humanity. Yet as we shall see later, the notion of power as our basic human motive, while intuitively attractive, has its share of skeptics. Even if it didn't, the puzzle would still remain: why power now?

The explanation, I think, concerns the impact of massive social change on the nature of culture. As a result of the two world wars, the end of colonialism, the information age and the process labeled globalization, with multinational corporations descending on Third World countries and political and economic migrants gravitating to the West, the world has not only become smaller, but it has also mutated in a manner of profound significance for anthropology: culture has been transformed. On the one hand, culture, whether in the Orient or the Occident, has been fragmented. The notion of a homogeneous, cohesive, geographically bounded local culture consisting of people who share a putative common ancestry is obsolete; cultures have now become multicultures, and the sheer repertoire of distinctive cultures, as Brumann (1998:499) has pointed out, has shrunk. On the other hand, a new form of culture has swept the world. Whether due to the convergence of different cultures towards a common middle point, or the enormous clout of Americanization, cultural similarity has everywhere been on the rise; this is to such an extent that some writers have speculated about an emerging global culture.

Emanating from the shock waves of the transformed nature of culture have been two dramatic shifts in the intellectual direction of the discipline, each of which has elevated the profile of power. The first of these, quite familiar to an anthropological audience, has been eagerly championed by some of us and indignantly rejected by others. I am referring to the no-holds-barred critique of the concept of culture during the past couple of decades. The argument, in part, is that the emphasis on cultural difference, long a celebrated feature of the discipline, has contributed to the oppression of non-Western peoples. Cultural difference allegedly has translated into inferiority, symbolized by the image of the unfortunate "Other."

The second intellectual change is equally revolutionary, for it disturbs the discipline's basic problematic. For most of the existence of the profession, that problematic has been as follows: how can the immense cultural diversity around the world be squared with the presumed underlying psychic and biological unity of Homo sapiens? What has not, in my view, been adequately appreciated is that social change has left that problematic behind. If human beings are similar not only in psychic and biological terms but also in cultural terms, the old problematic is no longer meaningful. As I shall argue later in some detail, a new problematic has emerged which almost reverses the old one. Instead of asking what unites human beings, given widespread cultural difference, it asks what divides them in a world of cultural similarity.

Both the critique of culture and the emergence of a new problematic have signalled a fundamental shift in anthropological orientation. Rather than being documented, celebrated and even created via the pursuit of the exotic, difference has been problematized and the door has been opened to a relative stranger in the discipline: power.

WRITING AGAINST CULTURE

Before jumping into the critique of culture, we should remind ourselves why the concept enjoyed such heroic stature in early anthropology, and continues to attract its share of defenders today. When Boas, the renowned founder of American anthropology, arrived on the scene, the evolutionary perspective dominated the intellectual atmosphere, biology was thought to explain human behavior, and race in the phenotypical sense of observed physical characteristics was the discipline's key concept, reflected in the hierarchically arranged taxonomies characteristic of the times.

The culture concept emerged to challenge existing thinking on two levels. One was that of the species, the other that of variation within the species, corresponding respectively to Culture (with a large "C") and culture (with a small "c"). The argument in the first instance was that Homo sapiens was not just another species. Instead it had a capacity for Culture. This was evident in language acquisition and symbolic thought (for example, Leslie White's famous remark that only human beings distinguish between holy water and ordinary water). Culture made Homo sapiens unique. To a degree not remotely matched by any other species, it was liberated from the dictates of biological programming. As Kroeber (1963:9; orig. 1923) remarked long ago: "There is no culture on the sub-human level." More recently Gamst and Norbeck (1976:4) commented: "only humans create and transmit culture."

The concept of culture, with a small "c," was equally significant. It emerged to plug a hole created by the demolition of the race concept. The prevailing argument, set in motion by the Boasians, was that there was only one human race. But if race is a constant, how could the widespread variation of "ways of life" around the world be explained and labelled? The answer was culture. Each of those ways of life was thought to represent a distinctive culture, with an identifiable language, geographical location, world view, and behavior. In other words, culture was a variable, irreducible to biology.

It was at this point that the notion of relativism, promoted by the Boasians, rose to the top of the anthropological agenda. In its milder form relativism conveyed a humanistic message. It insisted that all cultures are morally equal, and that the standards of one culture can't be used to judge what people think and do in another culture. Otherwise ethnocentrism would reign. In its more extreme form, relativism not only promoted the idea that each culture is unique, thus confounding cross-cultural analysis and scientific ambition, but also left the impression that when it comes to culture anything goes.

With culture as their key concept, and field workers busily filling in the ethnographic map, the basic problematic that was to dominate the discipline for most of its history came into focus. To repeat: how can the immense cultural variation around the globe be reconciled with the presumed psychic and biological unity of humankind? The answer, or rather the almost non-answer, was that such variation demonstrated the countless ways in which it was possible to be human. Indeed, each description of a previously unstudied culture was cause for celebration—sure proof of the autonomy of culture from biology and the irrelevancy of race.

The answer also took another form. Cultural difference prevailed on the surface, psychic and biological unity under the surface. This made it possible to promote the notion of cultural uniqueness while at the same time affirming that we all belong to a single species. Eventually a glimpse of another kind of underlying unity came into focus. As Bailey (1969:ix) put it: "Beneath the contextual variations and cultural differences, political behaviour reveals structural regularities." If we replace political by social behavior in general, we can argue that there are cross-cultural regularities beneath the surface in the sociological realm, not just in terms of mental and biological make-up. This legitimates the formulation of sociological types that cut across cultures, and thus the comparative framework as well.

Of course, there was a lot of fuzzy thinking going on at the time (and there still is). For example, biology (and race) was ruled out as the explanation of variation in "ways of life" because it was deemed to be a constant. But Culture, with a large "C," also was a species constant. How, then, did it operate as a variable?

On what logical principle was it possible to posit C/c simultaneously? There were other problems. As Kaplan and Manners (1972:5) point out, cultural uniqueness was not usually demonstrated, but rather accepted as a matter of faith. Could the same thing be said about the presumed psychic and biological unity of humankind? Well, Argyrou (1999) has recently argued that until the idea of "sameness" of all humanity was embraced, ethnology could not even be established as an independent discipline. But he added that it is simply not possible to demonstrate sameness, for it is a metaphysical assumption beyond empirical inquiry.

Argyrou's position notwithstanding, the idea of psychic unity has been firmed up by the investigations of a number of prominent scholars from Boas to Tylor, Frazer, Malinowski, Evans-Pritchard, and Lévi-Strauss. Indeed, those who dared, or seemed to dare, to challenge the reigning orthodoxy such as Lévy-Bruhl were virtually drummed out of the discipline. Lévy-Bruhl, a contemporary of Durkheim in France, distinguished between logical (or Western) and prelogical (or primitive) mentality. Western logic rested on the rule of non-contradiction, which stated that two objects can't occupy the same space at the same time. Prelogical mentality was not simply an elementary form of Western mentality, but instead a different mentality. It operated according to what Lévy-Bruhl called the law of participation, which meant that it did not attempt to avoid contradiction, and was infused with irrationality and mysticism. The cold shoulder given to Lévy-Bruhl conveyed a clear message: it was legitimate to distinguish between the primitive and the modern in sociological terms, as Durkheim had done with his distinction between mechanical and organic solidarity. But it was beyond the pale to question the panhuman unity of the mind's operations.[1]

Surprisingly, in view of the apparent victory of culture over race, the case for biological unity has been much less consistent. Boas was unrivalled in early anthropology for his vigorous opposition to racism (1910, 1940, 1962, 1963). He saw racism as a social and political phenomenon, and observed that racial taxonomies inevitably became converted into hierarchies. Yet as Visweswaran (1998:72) has pointed out, Boas also thought that race could be stripped of its pejorative connotations and serve as a legitimate scientific concept.[2]

Several years later the British social anthropologist Raymond Firth (1956) was taking much the same position. While quick to dismiss racial purity as political propaganda rather than a scientific concept, he apparently found nothing objectionable in referring to the Zulu as a separate race. Today it might be thought that the idea of separate races is ludicrous, embraced only by white supremacists. Yet as I shall show more fully in chapter three, recent research (Lieberman et al. 1992) indicates that at least half of the biologists and physical anthropologists surveyed in the 1980s continued to accept the concept of biological races within the species Homo sapiens.

From what we have seen so far, the concept of culture, important as it has been in the confrontation of racial thinking, was not unblemished even in the early days. But the massive critique that has emerged during the past couple of decades has approached the concept from another angle. Culture has been accused of creating difference where it did not exist, of transforming difference into inferiority for the benefit of the West, and even of taking on some of the properties of the very concept it was meant to replace: race.

From Abu-Lughod to Appadurai, Clifford, Fabian, Keesing and Said, the message has been consistent: culture is a conceptual tool, a discourse, that has generated and sustained the unequal relationship between the West and the non-West. Culture stereotypes, homogenizes, and essentializes "the Other," while ignoring change, conflict, and individual agency. In Whittaker's words (1992:113): "Culture is the very epitome of othering. It depends for its existence on the subjective ordering of a world full of Others." Similarly, Abu-Lughod (1991: 143) has written: "Culture is the essential tool for making other. As a professional discourse that elaborates on the meaning of culture in order to account for, explain, and understand cultural difference, anthropology also helps construct, produce and maintain it. Anthropololgical discourse gives cultural difference (and the separation between groups of people it implies) the air of the self-evident." So fundamental is the notion of "the Other" to anthropology that Keesing has argued (1994:301) that if "radical alterity did not exist, it would be anthropology's project to invent it."

Not only does culture allegedly promote timelessness, discreteness, homogeneity, holism, consensus, continuity, essentialism, and localism, but it also obfuscates power for the benefit of Western domination. Relativism itself may have been one of the culprits. By floating the idea of equality across supposed unique cultures, it diverted attention from the power imbalances among them, especially between the West and the Rest.

Now for the unkindest cut of all. This is the argument that culture has become a crude equivalent of race, the very concept it was meant to replace. Abu-Lughod, Kahn, Appadurai and Friedman, as Brumann (1999:2) has pointed out, have all taken this position. As Abu-Lughod (1991:144) put it: "Despite its anti-essentialist intent ... the culture concept retains some of the tendencies to freeze difference possessed by concepts like race." Kahn (1989:18–19) has argued that the traits used to designate differences between cultures are just as arbitrary as those used to identify races. According to Michaels (1992:684): "Our sense of culture is characteristically meant to displace race, but ... culture has turned out to be a way of continuing rather than repudiating racial thought." It was in this context that Visweswaran (1998:65 and 79) evoked the expression "cultural racism" and advised "that we not mourn the passing of the modern concept of culture."

These several criticisms are severe, and largely justifiable, but two or three clarifications are in order. A key question is whether the culture concept has always been flawed, or only became so in recent years as a result of social change. My view is that from the word go there have been troubling aspects to the concept. The assumptions of consensus, uniformity, and stability have been suspect, as well as the image of the bounded, discrete population. To take West

Africa as an example, a part of the world which I used to know well, when one referred to the Igbo, one had to ask which Igbo, because those who lived in Owerri were not the same in terms of social organization and beliefs and attitudes as those who lived in Abakaliki. As for the Yoruba, such was the complexity and variation of their political system that Peter Lloyd, who devoted much of his life to studying it (1960, 1968), once remarked that he could write an introductory textbook in political science while drawing all his examples from the Yoruba. In its own way West Africa was deterritorialized long before that term came into the discipline. Traders and adventurers, often speaking several languages, were constantly on the move, with Igbo and Yoruba communities popping up in the northern past of the Ivory Coast, and Hausa communities in Lagos and Enugu.

None of the above bears much resemblance to the classical portrait of culture. Nevertheless, in recent years, as a result of social change, culture has been transformed on a worldwide scale to a degree unmatched in previous history. As Appadurai (1991:191) has explained: "The landscapes of group identity—the ethnoscapes—around the world are no longer familiar anthropological objects, insofar as groups are no longer tightly territorialized, spatially bounded, historically unselfconscious, or culturally homogeneous."

Neither in the West nor the Rest do culture, ethnicity, and nation continue to jibe. With deterritorialization and transnationalism, I can now study the Nuer on the doorstep of the university in southern Ontario where I hang my hat, or the Yoruba in Toronto and the Igbo in Ottawa. My sense is that most of the recent critics of culture have had the classical form in mind. Yet the thrust of the critique fits much better with the fragmented portrait of culture that has emerged since World War II.

The argument that difference equals inferiority also can be questioned. The message today coming from governments and corporations often is exactly the opposite: difference is "cool." It is something not merely to respect but to rejoice in. Of course, the message itself may be less important than what prompted it. Widespread prejudice and discrimination may have set the government's propaganda machine in motion; and by arguing that we are one big family, multinational corporations might be able to sell more soap.

What about the attitudes of anthropologists? Rather than treating difference as inferiority, most of them, in my experience, regard the societies in the non-West in which they have conducted participant observation to be the superior ones, where human relationships are rich, rewarding and satisfying. Like the message from governments and corporations, however, the attitudes of anthropologists can be given a different spin. Such praise for the Third World might be little more than romanticism (if not paternalism), indirectly perpetuating the unequal power balance with the West for the sake of glorious tradition.

There also is the question of the origin of the culture concept. If I have left the impression that it emerged for one reason only—to banish race from the scene—that would be unfortunate. As Wolf (1999) has argued most stimulatingly, culture also owes its existence to the counter-Enlightenment, a term coined by Isaiah Berlin. The Enlightenment espoused rationality, universalism and a common humanity. The counter-Enlightenment opposed all of these, emphasizing instead primordialism, parochialism, particularism, uniqueness, spirit, and subjectivity. Culture (and society) was the term coined to capture the counter-Enlightenment sentiment. It could even be argued that the counter-Enlightenment reinforced the race concept. Reaction against the Enlightenment was especially pronounced in Germany, where the ideas of community, folk, and national destiny rested easily next to the notion of racial purity.

Before turning to the new problematic, let me make a few observations about the impact of the critique of culture on my anthropological colleagues. Their reactions have been all over the map. In one camp are those who want to scrap the culture concept. Clifford (1988:274) has mused that the concept may have served its time, while Abu-Lughod (1991) recommends that it be replaced by concepts which highlight rather than hide hierarchy and power, such as Said's discourse and Bourdieu's practice. Fabian (1991:261–262) has gone a step further. Mounting the now familiar argument that anthropology was the child of imperialism, he has declared that not just culture but anthropology in general should disappear from the academic scene. This will transpire, he suggests, when the forces that created imperialism wither away, and rather than lamenting the demise of the discipline, anthropologists should help to dig its grave.

In a second camp are those who generally are in agreement with the critique, but nevertheless are reluctant to give culture the boot, not least of all because it has for so long defined the discipline of anthropology, at least on the American scene. One suggestion has been that culture as a noun be dropped, because it smacks of reification and essentialism, and cultural as an adjective be encouraged (Keesing 1994, Brumann 1999).

Complicating the picture has been the manner in which culture has been received beyond the academic world. One of the great ironies of our times is that just at the point when culture has been beaten up by the experts, it has been latched onto by lay people as one of the explanatory keys to their daily lives. Nowadays it is difficult to pick up a newspaper or watch television without seeing or hearing a reference to culture, such as the culture of the Republican camp or the Democratic camp, or the culture of weekend football fans. In this context, the fact that culture has emerged as the basis for legal defense in the courts is not without significance. As Brumann (1999:11) has stated: "Whether anthropologists like it or not, it appears that people—and not only those with power—*want* culture, and they often want it in precisely the bounded, reified, essentialized, and timeless fashion that most of us now reject." Once again, there is divided opinion as to whether the popularity of culture beyond the academy is a good or a bad thing. In Gingrich's view, that is another reason for dumping the concept, because lay people will simply perpetuate the mistakes of the past made by the experts. Yet Hannerz counters that if it were dumped, the credibility of the discipline in the eyes of the public would suffer.[3]

Muddying the waters even more is the stature of culture in the Third World. As Keesing (1994:303 and 307) has pointed out, culture has been seized by Third World elites and used as nationalist rhetoric: "We have a culture, we are special, we are a people." In other words, Third World elites have turned the tables on anthropology, evoking the old essentialized and reified conception of culture to promote national goals and criticize foreign scholars who attempt to steal their culture while never really understanding it. It is in this context, perhaps, that Herzfeld (1997:192) highlighted the state's effort to promote a sense of national cultural identity so as to counteract divisions and anomy at the community level. Of course, this is not a political ploy confined to the Third World. In Canada, both multiculturalism and bilingualism have been criticized (see Moodley 1981 and Peter 1981) as tools for propping up the dominance of the ruling English elite and obfuscating the lack of power held by other ethnic groups.

Finally, I should indicate that reactions to the critique of culture have produced a third camp, although it won't be described in detail until Chapter Three. It consists of scholars who are up in arms about the alleged flaws in the culture concept. From their perspective the critique is nothing more than a fabrication which has distorted the wide variety of ways in which culture has been conceptualized since the days of Boas (see Boddy and Lambek 1997). These scholars reject the charge that anthropologists have dwelled almost entirely on difference, or have treated such difference as inferiority. For the people in this camp, culture has been and continues to be anthropology's superstar.

REFINING THE PROBLEMATIC

By the 1960s it was clear that anthropology was in a state of crisis, unsure of its long-presumed mandate as the academic discipline that specialized in other cultures. Out of this crisis emerged a proliferation of theoretical approaches, most of them determined to kill off structural functionalism once and for all, as well as a spate of self-indulgent doomsday books documenting and lamenting the demise of the discipline.

Why the crisis? The conventional explanation is that it was brought about by massive social change (and possibly by growing frustration that the discipline's scientific ambitions were not being realized). I agree that social change was at the core of the crisis, but the precise impact of the crisis on anthropology has never, to my knowledge, been clearly stated: the crisis was the first signal that our old problematic had lost much of its relevance. Primitive society, on which anthropology fed, and colonial society, on which it grew fat, were things of the past.

Modernization, or Westernization, was in the air, rivalled by the socialist model of development, both agendas pointing to a more uniform society as distinctive structures and values withered in the face of industrialization. If all this suggested that the world might be shrinking, globalization removed any lingering doubts. Indeed globalization, in the guise of multinational corporations and deterritorialization, provided the final push that toppled the old problematic from its perch. It no longer made sense to ask how widespread cultural variation can be reconciled with underlying psychic and biological unity if local cultures were fragmented and cultural similarity was sweeping the globe.

The same forces of social change that undermined the old problematic gave birth to its replacement. Human beings share not only mental and biological make-up, but increasingly cultural make-up as well. Yet they are still divided. The question is why? This leads to a focus on stratification and its principal components: class, gender, ethnicity, and race. It also brings power into the center of the picture, because it is embedded in these components.

The new problematic is almost tantamount to the old problematic run backwards. Instead of asking what unites people, it asks what keeps them apart. In the old problematic difference was assumed to exist on the surface, sameness under the surface. In the new problematic similarity exists on the surface, and difference beneath the surface: the expression of power struggles for advantage. Of course, when these struggles are blatant, they too rise to the surface, observable to all of us. Yet in the normal state of affairs the forces that generate difference are concealed by ideologies that evoke justice and equality. It should be added that even in the era of globalization cultural difference at the surface level persists to some degree, and is especially pronounced in the nooks and crannies where power is weak, fostered by nations attempting to ward off globalization and by ethnic groups struggling for identity and self-esteem.

Under the old problematic, cultural difference was almost treated as a natural phenomenon to be documented and celebrated. Under the new problematic difference is a social and political product reflecting advantage and disadvantage. In other words, difference is problematized. Rather than taking for granted the existence of distinctive cultures, and then asking how we can encourage conversations across them, as Geertz does, we ask how such difference was produced in the first place, and we look for the answer at the world system level.[4] An early effort along these lines was Frank's thesis (1966) that "underdevelopment" was "developed" by Western society. The political dimension of difference is indicated in Clifford's remark (1988:14): "'Cultural' difference is no longer a stable, exotic otherness; self-other relations are matters of power and rhetoric rather than essence." An even closer expression of the new problematic has been articulated by Gupta and Ferguson (1992:14): "We are interested less in establishing a dialogic relation between geographically distinct societies than in exploring the process of *production* of difference in a world of culturally, socially, and economically interconnected and interdependent spaces." Later they comment (p.16): "if we question a pre-given world of separate and discrete 'peoples and cultures,' and see instead a difference-producing set of relations, we turn from a project of juxtaposing preexisting differences to one of exploring the construction of differences in historical processes."

The obvious question is whether the new problematic leaves any room for culture, a question raised about a wide range of theoretical perspectives from

Malinowski's manipulative Trobrianders to Wallerstein's world system model. If what we have in mind is culture in the classical sense of homogeneity, discreteness, and god-like explanatory omnipotence, the answer is no. The same holds true for the textbook rendition of culture as shared, learned, and transmitted by socialization from one generation to another; the world has become too complex to accommodate that neat formula. However, even if a new problematic has emerged, human beings will continue to distinguish holy water from ordinary water, and tradition, at least fragments of tradition, will still have an impact on social interaction, as will ideas, values, normative expectations, and ideology. These are a few of the ingredients of what we normally mean by culture. While some anthropologists might argue that we hardly need a cover term—culture—for them, anthropological investigation without them is difficult to imagine, even if they play second fiddle to power.

ARGUMENTS FOR SIMILARITY

Half a century ago Lévi-Strauss (1974; orig. 1955) peeked over the horizon and announced what he saw: monoculture on the march. More recently, in response to a question about whether humanity is moving towards total uniformity, he stated (1994:421): "Total is too strong a word. But never has it been possible to speak so convincingly of global civilization as it is today." The same message is offered by Bennett (1987:47): "Regardless of what is happening to local cultures, people of the world over are learning to accept common mental images of the meaning of life and the nature of human survival." Consistent with this observation are the words of Clifford (1988:14): "One no longer leaves home confident of finding something radically new, another time or space. Difference is encountered in the adjoining neighbourhood, the familiar turns up at the ends of the earth." Or as Trouillot put it (1991:19): "On sheer empirical grounds, the differences between Western and non-Western societies are blurrier than ever before. Anthropology's answer to this ongoing transformation has been typically ad hoc and haphazard."

Unsystematic the adjustment of anthropology may have been, but it was adjustment nonetheless. Even before World War II, social change had begun to be a focus of study, with conflict and agency soon to join it, and later gender, ethnicity, and class. Along the way many of the famous dichotomies such as simple vs. complex, illiterate vs. literate, folk vs. urban, Toennies' Gemeinschaft–Gesellschaft divide, and Parsons' pattern variables were quietly dropped. The reason was that they were intended to capture differences between "them" and "us" which no longer existed. In more recent years, in response to globalization, attention has turned to questions about identity, self, and community. The implication is that anthropologists all along have been conducting investigations which recognize that the world has changed, and are consistent with the refined problematic. All that I have done, then, is to make explicit what previously was implicit. This in itself may not lack importance if the "ad hoc and haphazard" reaction of anthropologists is replaced by the systematic investigation of difference laced with power.

ARGUMENTS FOR NEW FORMS OF DIFFERENCE

The question of the hour, as Appadurai (1990:295) has observed, is whether cultural homogeneity or cultural heterogeneity now describes the world. The overwhelming consensus among anthropologists, as Brumann (1998) has pointed out, is that cultural homogeneity has not materialized. It is not that they disagree with the evidence in support of growing cultural similarity. Rather the argument, at least in its sophisticated form, is that globalization divides as it unites, generating not only cultural similarity, but also new forms of diversity.

Representative of the prevailing anthropological position is Hannerz, who has stated (1992:218): "It must now be more difficult than ever, or at least more unreasonable, to see the world . . . as a cultural mosaic, of separate pieces with hard, well-defined edges. Cultural interconnections increasingly reach across the world. More than ever, there is a global ecumene." This would appear to support the homogeneity position, but elsewhere he has written (1990:237): "There now is a world culture, but we had better make sure that we understand what that means. It is marked by an organization of diversity rather than by a replication of uniformity. No total homogenization of systems of meaning and expression has occurred, nor does it appear likely that there will be one any time soon."

Sometimes the rejection of global uniformity consists of little more than a bald-faced denial that it has occurred. Thus Featherstone (1995:114) declares that globalization does not mean "a unified society or culture." At other times the argument seems to float on wishes and dreams. Clifford (1988:15–16), referring to his "utopian, persistent hope for the reinvention of difference," concludes rather dogmatically: "The future is not (only) monoculture." Lévi-Strauss (1994:421) asks: "who knows whether new differences will not appear among a humanity that is in great danger of losing its diversity." Then there is the argument that the homogeneity position should be rejected because *total* global cultural uniformity—a universal culture comparable to the nation-state (a world government?)—has not been achieved. Yet who in their right minds would ever expect such an outcome? It is much more reasonable to ask about the degree to which cultural uniformity has spread around the globe, and whether anything comparable to it has been seen before. Because global cultural uniformity often has been interpreted as Americanization—the cocacolonization of the world, cultural dumping of old drugs and movies—one can almost sense the relief behind the conclusion that cultural heterogeneity is still alive and well, even if only because other centers of cultural dominance and dispersion such as Japan, China, and Vietnam rival the American one.

More sophisticated by far is the argument that globalization creates new forms of diversity. Good examples are transnational cultures, people from the homeland interacting in the diaspora, their identity and world view stretched across continents. Then there is the state of affairs that has been labelled indigenization or creolization. What this means is that when a cultural item from one part of the world winds up in another, it is reshaped by its new cultural setting. In this context it is important to remember that cultural goods don't flow only from the West to the East. The reverse also occurs, and with similar signs of creolization. For example, Burke (1999) has shown that Eastern cosmetics and clothing adopted by Western consumers take on meanings, and are even physically altered, to render them consistent with their new environment.

Diversity also is maintained, so it is argued, because globalization unleashes new forms of opposition. Earlier I referred to the tendency of Third World elites to fight back by promoting precisely the reified, essentialized version of culture now rejected by many anthropologists. Wallerstein (see King 1990:408) points to nationalism as the form that resistance to globalization takes. Of course, there is little new in that interpretation, since Marx said much the same thing. Marx and Engels, as Omi and Winant (1986:45) have indicated, actually held contradictory views about the impact of capitalism. On the one hand they argued that as capitalism stretched over the entire globe, nations and national boundaries would cease to be meaningful. On the other hand they thought that the spread of capitalism itself generated increased nationalism as capitalist powers struggled among themselves for world control, oppressed nations tried to resist, and efforts were made to detract attention within nations from class antagonisms.

Several other arguments could be marshalled to support diversity, even while accepting that cultural uniformity on a global scale has reached a height unattained in previous history. Mass protests at the turn of the millennium against globalization and multinational corporations, accused of benefiting from the labor power and natural resources of Third World nations, and of driving the wedge between rich and poor in the industrialized world even deeper, could be interpreted as a sign that another counter-Enlightenment movement is gathering steam. In the 1960s convergence theory was in the air, more of interest to sociologists than to anthropologists. Although a few writers argued that convergence, especially between industrialized nations in the West and the Soviet bloc, was indeed occurring, most commentators were skeptical (Weinberg 1969). It is an open question whether there is anything about globalization that would change their minds today, especially if the position taken by the majority of anthropologists is anything to go by. Even if the evidence for a new form of culture—cultural similarity on a global level—is highly persuasive, which I think is the case, that doesn't mean the world has become a simpler place. Long ago Durkheim distinguished between mechanical and organic solidarity. I have never liked the term *solidarity*, and would substitute *complexity* for it, partly as a foil to assumptions about consensus and stability, and partly to remind us that in their own way preindustrial societies were as complex as industrialized societies. My argument is that in recent decades a new kind of complexity has emerged, which I shall label global complexity. The distance between organic and global complexity is just as great as that between mechanical and organic complexity. And wherever complexity is found, can diversity be far behind?

Sticking to Durkheim, we might also remember his argument that as structural and role differentiation take place in society, a function partly of social density in his writings, new forms of overarching structure inevitably emerge. The pattern of fission and fusion is integral to human social organization, at least in Durkheim's muted evolutionary (in contradistinction to his loud structural functional) perspective, and arguably another source of diversity in the era of globalization.

It could even be claimed that diversity is a mental phenomenon, something carried around in people's heads, despite being at odds with empirical reality. That is, unique local cultures have crumbled, but people's imagined sense of such cultures has not. As Gupta and Ferguson (1992:10) put it: "The irony of these times is that as actual places and localities become even more blurred and indeterminate, *ideas* of culturally and ethnically distinct places become perhaps even more salient." And Brumann (1998:500) has remarked: "it may well be that people are becoming more alike while feeling more unlike."

Before closing the book on the homogeneity–heterogeneity debate, let us turn to some of Brumann's ideas on the subject. In his judgment, nationalism, ethnicity, and kinship all oppose the homogenizing tendency in globalization. Yet he is reluctant to place himself alongside the majority view that diversity prevails. One of his reasons is that anthropologists have a vested interest in promoting cultural uniqueness. Another reason is that nobody really knows much about the balance between homogeneity and heterogeneity simply because so little solid research has been done on the subject. Brumann then goes on to make an argument which should cause his colleagues to have indigestion. He suggests that while global homogenization has not occurred in realms such as religion and identity, it has penetrated politics, the economy, administration, technology, science, and medicine. In his words (1998:500): "It appears likely that a strong tendency of homogenization dominates the 'harder' cultural domains while others remain comparatively free of it." When I first read these words, a vision of Julian Steward's core-periphery model (1955) flashed before my eyes. Steward's core consists of the "hard" elements of social life. The core is where independent variables are found and causality unfolds. The periphery is home to the "soft" elements: leisure, fads, fashions. The periphery can vary relatively independent of the core for the simple reason that it bears little weight on the trajectory of society. If Brumann is correct that it is the harder parts of the sociocultural domain that have been homogenized, it hardly matters whether new forms of difference have emerged or not. They are bound eventually to be overwhelmed by the homogenized core.

CONCLUSION

Power, as D'Andrade (1999:96) has put it so well, is the new god-term in anthropology but could it just be a fad, or at least less important regardless of how long it remains at the top than many of us seem to think? Academic disciplines have always been vulnerable to the notion of a master concept or explanation, be it the environment, technology, or sex. With culture down for the count, power stepped into the ring—the knock-down explanation we demand. There is an even more disturbing possibility. A remarkable overlap exists between the writings for and against culture and the old debate between consensus and conflict models. The sense of belonging, the shared values, the stability, and the overall integration and equilibrium associated with the consensus model were also principal components in the culture concept in early anthropology. The divided interests, inequality, and change inherent in the conflict model resonate with the critique of culture mounted by Abu-Lughod and company. The reason why this is troubling is that it seems to support an argument that I mounted several years ago (Barrett 1984), namely that shifts in theoretical orientation do not come about merely as responses to social change, or because a better explanation has emerged. Instead, they respond in part to a number of elementary oppositions such as consensus vs. conflict and stability vs. change which are embedded deep within the discipline's conceptual scheme and are never resolved. When consensus dominates one theoretical orientation it is probable that conflict will surface in its successor, only to be dislodged at a future date. This helps to explain why theory in the discipline has been repetitive rather than cumulative.

If the critique of culture was the only source of the switch to power, it would be difficult not to conclude that the battle between those in favor of and opposed to the culture concept is simply the latest manifestation of the consensus–conflict debate. But there was another source: the transformed problematic, itself a product of massive social change, capped by the globalization process. This makes it more likely that the focus on power indeed is justifiable and significant.

The turn toward power also was brought about by various innovative theoretical perspectives such as postmodernism and feminist anthropology. Both show how systems of domination are sustained by discourses which reinforce authority and representation. Each of them sketches out the mechanics of resistance, such as by being dialogical and polyvocal, but in my judgment the feminist approach does the job better. This is partly because feminist anthropology, as Mascia-Lees et al. (1989) state, knows its politics, whereas it is never quite clear whether the egalitarian-oriented, relativistic-loving postmodernists are out to save the world or to save their own skins.[5]

Another source of the focus on power was the growing impact of counter-disciplines such as cultural studies, multicultural studies and ethnic studies. By no means can it be said that these three share a common vision of the world, or support each other's efforts to challenge conventional scholarship. As Rosaldo (1994:527) has indicated, mainstream anthropologists might resent cultural studies for claiming partial ownership over the culture concept, but those in ethnic studies have a more serious complaint; they regard cultural studies as little more than an attempt to replace them by the authority of white males. To the extent that this charge is valid, surely it applies to multicultural studies as well. Where the three counter-disciplines do come together is in the relationship assumed between culture and power. As Keesing (1994:303) has remarked, what separates cultural studies from cultural anthropology "is the stress in cultural studies on the articulation of symbolic systems with class and power–the production and reproduction of cultural forms." As Rosaldo has put it (1994:525), in culture studies "culture is laced with power and power is shaped by culture." In multiculturalism studies, culture seems to be a means to an end, not an end in itself as in mainstream anthropology (Turner 1993). Culture is a basis for resistance and empowerment. And it is culture in its reified sense. As Eller (1997:252) has said about the multicultural approach: "Groups appear to fight *about* culture, but actually fight *with* culture. Culture is a group's seal of authenticity and its warranty of worth, serving as a gloss, a badge, and a weapon for a party in the war of *identity* politics."

In all three counter-disciplines, power is integrated with culture to a degree not remotely matched in mainstream anthropology. Hannerz (1997:542–543), however, urges caution about the culture-as-empowerment theme. While culture can be a source of pride and consciousness-raising, and a resource in the struggle for advantage in the broader political arena, it can also be used to identify and demonize groups (cultural cleansing), as we know only too well from the case of Bosnia.

In view of the critique of culture, the transformed problematic, and the emergence of power as a central focus, it seems likely that we shall have to rethink where we are heading in terms of theory. Consider the competing perspectives provided by Harris and Geertz. Harris has advocated a scientific style of inquiry, with the emphasis on etics rather than emics. His cultural materialist approach embraces evolution and ecology, and promotes general anthropology, or a synthesis of physical anthropology, archaeology, linguistics, and cultural anthropology. He has attempted nothing less than to map the global trends in stratification from the earliest humans to the present. Geertz, in contrast, at least in his later years, has put the emphasis on interpretation, subjectivity, and particularism. With "thick description" as the slogan, he has strived for the deep penetration of individual cases, eschewed generalization across them, and advocated treating culture as the equivalent of a literary text, thus presaging the turn toward postmodernism.

If anthropologists were asked who won the battle between Harris and Geertz, surely it would be no contest: Geertz has been the top dog on the American scene. Yet if I am on the right track regarding the new problematic and the importance of power, it would appear that the fortunes of these two renowned scholars are about to be reversed. That is, Harris's star (or at least the approach he represents) is going to rise. This is because to a much greater degree than in the case of Geertz, his perspective accommodates institutionalized inequality, or structural differences shaped by power. That forecast (or educated guess) will be reinforced if post-positivism slowly withers away, which I expect to happen, and positivism reclaims the center of the discipline.[6] Geertz, of course, has not been inattentive to social change, or to political and economic dimensions, especially in earlier works like *Peddlars and Princes*. What this may mean is that a partial synthesis of Harris and Geertz may be possible, constructed around the theme of stratification.

With the focus on stratification, anthropology once and for all has been catapulted into the modern world. Longings for the good old days when cultures were cultures, and doubts whether the discipline can survive without a world full of primitives (or at least "Others"), should now be behind us. It used to be said back in the 1960s, when I first discovered anthropology, that stratification might be the issue around which the social sciences would be unified. Could it be that its time finally has come? One thing is certain. We have arrived at a stage in history where it is increasingly improbable that an ethnography of a distinctive people or culture is going to surprise anyone because of its stunning uniqueness and exotic nature. In other words, anthropology's old trump card no longer will do the trick.

I have placed a lot of weight on globalization as the tool that finally buried the old problematic and uncovered power. It could be argued, however, that there is nothing new about globalization. After all, there were the colonial empires of the past, and trading entities such as the East India Company that seemed to operate in a manner similar to today's multinational corporations. Yet these former imperialisms, as Smith (1990:176) has pointed out, were tied to their places of origin, be it Britain, France, or Spain. In contrast, globalization today is more or less anchorless. To some degree it has superseded the nation-state. In Smith's words, it is "supranational," quite possibly "universal," and "essentially memoryless" in terms of cultural, national, or geographic origin.

By forcing us to rethink our basic problematic, globalization (and earlier social change) may have put an end to the crisis that had dogged the steps of anthropology since the 1960s. This does not mean, however, that a single, dominant theoretical orientation is about to emerge, or that paradigmatic status will be achieved. That pleasant state of affairs never existed even when the old problematic was at the height of its influence. But it may mean that there will be a sense of direction to the discipline and a degree of confidence among its practitioners unknown since the days of Radcliffe-Brown, Gluckman, and Steward.

NOTES

1. Littleton, in a long introduction to a new edition of Lévy-Bruhl's *How Natives Think* (1985; orig. 1910), argues that Lévy-Bruhl has been unfairly criticized, pointing out that he did not contend that "the natives" were always, or even normally, lost in a fog of mys-

ticism, and that he also argued that mystical thinking was found in Western thought. Lévy-Bruhl's mistake, Littleton suggests, was to generalize prelogical mentality across the range of primitive society. This contradicted both the relativistic assumption that each society has its own form of mentality, and that at a deeper level the operations of the human brain were universal.

2. It is interesting that Ruth Benedict, a cultural anthropologist and one of Boas's most prominent students, shared his opinion that *race* could be a serviceable scientific concept, while the physical anthropologist Ashley Montagu, another of his students, argued that the race concept could never be freed from its negative connotations, and should be replaced by *ethnic group*.

I might also point out that even the mighty Boas has been accused in recent years of harboring racist attitudes (see Fried 1972:61 and Willis 1969:139).

3. Gingrich and Hannerz made these observations in the "Comments" section on Brumann's 1999 article.

4. The renewed (or extreme) relativism promoted by Geertz and the postmodernists might well be regarded as a last-gasp effort to keep the old problematic alive.

5. Here I am thinking of the charge (see Singer 1993:23 and Sangren 1988:408–409) that postmodernism is merely academic sport, or a power play mounted by white males in the academy to ward off threats to their privilege unleashed by social change.

6. This is a forecast, not a statement of my preference regarding positivism and postpositivism. In my view, there has been much to applaud about feminist anthropology and postmodernism, especially the attention paid to power.

Chapter 2

Conceptualizing Power

Power is an aphrodisiac. At least that's what one of my relatives blurted out when she learned that I was writing on the subject. If that was all there was to power, my job in this chapter would be considerably simpler, and a lot more fun. Sex, however, seems to have been the furthest thing from the minds of anthropologists and other scholars who have examined power. Indeed, some of the literature could serve as a substitute for a cold shower. While hoping that this chapter won't have a similar effect, I shall attempt to show how power has been conceptualized in anthropology over the years, and in other disciplines as well. With the latter in mind, considerable attention will be given to the high points in philosophy, political science and sociology, and to key figures such as Mills, Parsons, and Foucault.

BASIC CONCEPTS, DEFINITIONS AND ASSUMPTIONS

Power, authority, influence, persuasion, manipulation, and coercion (or force) constitute the basic terms in this field of inquiry. To these we could add a secondary list reflecting particular theoretical orientations and political types: band, tribe, and state; factions, political arenas and political fields; domination and ideology; hegemony, habitus, discourse, and resistance; and of course perennial dualisms such as power vs. authority, formal vs. informal power, intentional vs. unintentional power, and elitism vs. pluralism. Depending on the investigator's theoretical and ethnographic interests, any one of the basic terms could be nominated as the key term. Thus, F.G. Bailey (1980), a field worker who has devoted much of his academic life to the study of politics at the micro, informal level, favors persuasion. From C. Wright Mills' perspective (1967:23), aimed at the macro level of society and state, coercion does the trick, augmented by manipulation and authority. My own inclination is to treat power as the master concept, with the other basic terms subsumed under it. This makes sense, I suggest, in relation to power's current high profile. It is hard to imagine a situation in which authority, influence, or any of the other terms could have challenged culture as our key concept. Only power appears to have the magnetism to shift the polar direction of the discipline.

Multiple, ambiguous, and even contradictory definitions of concepts are the norm in the social sciences, as any one who has looked into community or class (and of course culture) will know only too well. Power is no exception. For Hobbes (1971:2) power is "man's present means to any future apparent good," and for Russell (1938:35) "the production of intended effects." Harris (1971:415) defines it as follows: "Power is control over man and nature." Nicholas (1976:52) states: "'Power' is control over resources, whether human or material," while for Bailey (1980:3) "power is the capacity to make people do things, whether or not they wish it." Of course, implicit definitions can be extracted from slogans such as *power comes out of the barrel of a gun* and *the pen is mightier than the sword,* and from expressions such as *puppy power* and *pussy power.*

Contributing to the variety of definitions are several competing assumptions about the nature of power:

1. Power as a personality attribute.
2. Power as a substance, a thing, a force, something that can be grasped or harnessed, or allowed to slip away.
3. Power as a social relationship.
4. Structural power.

Most anthropologists today reject the first two assumptions. The argument is that power only makes sense in terms of interaction or social context. Thus one person may be powerful in relation to another person, but weak in relation to a third. This line of thinking, of course, reflects conventional disciplinary boundaries. Not surprisingly, psychologists have examined power as a personality attribute independent of social interaction (McClelland 1975, Winter 1973).

Power as a social relationship represents the Weberian perspective. His famous definition (1947:152) is that power is the capacity of an individual to impose his or her will on another individual despite resistance. This often is referred to as the zero-sum view of power, because one gains power at the expense of someone else. In Weber's approach, power is intentional and subjective, with priority given to agency rather than structure. Structural power is thought to be unintentional and objective in that advantage and disadvantage are products of the shape of the institutional framework of society—for example, whether patrimony prevails or free labor or slavery—independent of human volition. Marx's name often is attached to the structural model of power. In my view this is somewhat misleading because it ignores the quasi-independent role that he assigns to agency within the institutional framework of society.

It should be added that most writers would agree with Bohannan (1963:268–269) that power is an "aspect of all social relationships, whether it is exploited or not." The only opinion to the contrary that I have come across is that of Brown (1996), who dismissed that claim as meaningless and unprovable.

CONTRIBUTION OF ANTHROPOLOGY

In order to understand what has been happening in political anthropology, a dividing line has to be drawn between the long stretch of positivism from the beginnings of professional anthropology up to the 1970s, and the post-positivist phase that succeeded it. Dominating the first phase were the structural model and the processual model, with a third approach—the political economy model—hovering in the background. Emerging in the second phase was a new slant on power and authority which focused on discourse and representation; it turned the spotlight on anthropologists themselves, particularly the manner in which their ethnographic texts and key concepts such as culture had unwittingly reinforced global power imbalances.

THE STRUCTURAL MODEL

There is general agreement (see Claessen 1979:10) that political anthropology emerged as a specialized field of study in 1940, the year that Fortes and Evans-Pritchard published their edited volume on eight societies under the title *African Political Systems.* These societies were divided into two groups. The first had "centralized authority, administrative machinery, and judicial institutions—in short, a government—and in which cleavages of wealth, privilege, and status correspond to the distribution of power and authority." The second was characterized by the absence of "centralized authority, administrative machinery, and constituted judicial institutions," lacked "government" and had "no sharp divisions of rank, status, or wealth" (Fortes and Evans-Pritchard 1940:5).

Thus was born one of the most famous dichotomies in anthropology, variably described as stateless societies vs. societies with states, and societies without rulers vs. societies with rulers; perhaps just to bug us, the distinction also began to be referred to by the jargonistic terms acephalous and non-acephalous societies.

No doubt the evidence that there were indigenous states in Africa helped to dislodge the stereotype of simplicity. The notion of acephalous, leaderless societies was possibly even more significant, not least of all because of the argument that such societies very definitely were not in a state of anarchy. The reason was that while they lacked a centralized authority structure, they did not lack a capacity for political decision-making. These societies were organized in terms of lineages. The lineage system not only performed political functions, but it also was the principal source of equilibrium. Opposing lineages and sub-lineages, and the loyalties they engendered, balanced each other out, resulting in overall cohesion and stability.[1]

A great deal of excitement surrounded the publication of *African Political Systems*, but criticism eventually caught up with it.[2] Lloyd (1967) pointed out that the differences between societies with centralized authority and stateless societies were greatly exaggerated, especially by ignoring lineage in the first and dwelling on almost nothing but lineage in the second. Similarly, Cohen and Middleton (1967) argued that so-called acephalous and non-acephalous elements often were found in the same society, while Bohannan (1963) pointed out that even in acephalous societies it was not always lineage that performed the functions of politics; among the Hopi, for example, that responsibility resided in ritual and religious groups. The implication was that acephalous societies were considerably more varied and complex than represented in *African Political Systems*. That message was reinforced by the publication of *Tribes without Rulers* (Middleton and Tait 1958). Although it focused on six politically uncentralized societies in Africa which had segmentary lineage systems, the authors made it clear that there was a range of complexity in such societies beyond those organized in terms of lineage.

The most far-reaching criticism, however, was that *African Political Systems* was too closely tied to the structural-functional model that dominated the times (Radcliffe-Brown wrote the book's preface). Both types of society stressed equilibrium, structure and pattern, consensus and stability. As Sally Falk Moore (1994:374) observed about the early British structural functionalists in general, they emphasized order and coherence in order to show how logical the natives were; but these same elements arguably helped to hold colonialism together.

The Processual Model

In the 1960s what might loosely be labelled a paradigmatic shift took place in political anthropology. The focus switched from structure and function to process and event, and along the way new models of society and the actor were generated. The image of the social structure as a well-oiled machine humming along smoothly, or a healthy organism in a state of harmonious equilibrium, gave way to one that emphasized conflict, change, and irregularity. The actor ceased to be a robot controlled by society, materializing instead as a goal-oriented, choice-making, manipulative entrepreneur whose actions shaped a porous and ever-changing social structure. Political activity was considered to be the purposeful pursuit of and competition over public goals. In some respects, politics was thought to be comparable to a game. Coalitions, teams and cliques were made and unmade as people strived for advantage in the political arena. A basic assumption was that a huge gap existed between the institutionalized roles and

formal rules of the political system–how it ought to work–and the actual manner in which power was exercised. Bailey went as far as to argue that when it
comes to politics the formal realm is almost insignificant compared to the informal realm. This is not only because power is largely exercised outside of the
formal rules, but also because these rules themselves are manipulated by people for their own gratification. As Bailey put it (1980:4–5): "The successful com-
petitor is the one who manipulates regulations in his own favor, rather than
being bound by them. Those who play the game by the rules are apt to lose it.
A study of the use of power in a formal organization relying exclusively for its
information on the design of that organization, would touch only a small part
of the actual exercise of power within that organization."

This new perspective, variably labelled *the processual model, the transactional
model,* and *the interactional model,* added up to a massive attack on structural
functionalism. Rather than assuming a close correspondence between the normative order and behavioral patterns, as Durkheim had done, it painted a picture of inconsistent and contradictory norms and of choice-making individuals
manipulating the norms and deviating from them in the pursuit of self-interest.[3]
This perspective could also be called *the social action model* because it over-
lapped with Weber's conception of meaningful social action, in which a person
decides on a course of behavior in the context of her or his understanding of
what another person's reaction will be. I might add that Weber's zero-sum model
of power was the preferred approach among the transactionalists.

Anthropologists didn't have to go back to Weber in order to move beyond
structural functionalism. M.G. Smith (see Cohen and Middleton 1967:x) had divided government into *administration* and *politics.*[4] The first referred to institutionalized positions, regulations and hierarchies, the second to the give-and-
take among power-seeking individuals and the coalitions which they often
formed. This brings us to the subject of factions, which figured prominently in
the transactional literature. Factions are not corporate groups, nor are they permanent (Nicholas 1965). Rather they are political associations, based on personal ties between leader and follower which compete for prizes deemed to be
unclaimed, or at least vulnerable to counterclaims by ambitious and clever opponents. Factions, according to Nicholas (1976:58; orig. 1966), are often found
in environments undergoing rapid social change, where the normative framework has been loosened, and they tend to disappear when political associations
expand beyond the face-to-face level.

Factions fit very well—perhaps too well—into the processual model, inviting
the observation that they might have been focused on to the exclusion of other
types of political association. But that isn't the main criticism that has been directed at this model. The charge is that by being fixated on the micro politics of
everyday behavior, the more significant historical and structural forces external
to and encapsulating individual and local behavior are ignored. Thus Asad attacked Barth's factional interpretation of Swat Pathan politics (see Keesing
1976:363–365) for failing to appreciate that the outcome was largely dictated by

pre-existing exploitative economic relations. In Asad's perspective, individual consciousness, rather than being an independent and critical variable in human interaction, is a product of the class system.

We are confronted once again with one of those problems that just won't leave anthropology alone—the macro–micro dilemma. How does one pull off a study that is rich in local detail, and yet integrated into the broader historical and structural setting? Ironically, as the transactionalists caught their second wind (see Swartz 1976, and Tiffany 1979), they rethought their opposition to social structure, and came to the conclusion that both process and structure can be accommodated within a single framework. As Swartz (1968:8) pointed out about Bailey, a key figure in the transactional school (see *Stratagems and Spoils* 1969), that had been his position all along.

Other Models

While the structural and processual models undoubtedly dominated the positivistic era, a third model—political economy—lingered on the sidelines, at least in anthropology. Eric Wolf's earlier publications such as *Peasants* (1966) and *Peasant Wars of the Twentieth Century* (1969) were representative of this model, as was Fried's work on the state (1967), which I shall discuss later. I am also inclined to place part of Marvin Harris's cultural materialism under this model, especially works such as *Cows, Pigs, Wars, and Witches* (1975) where his evolutionary and general anthropology interests are less pronounced. Political economy is based on the reasonable assumption that the realms of politics and economics are intertwined, and together are driving forces of society and culture. This is the fundamental message in Wolf's impressive study, *Europe and the People without History* (1982). Wolf laments the differentiation of the various social sciences from political economy, and promotes a historically informed, Marxian-oriented approach which treats cultures and societies as parts of an integrated world system. Although Wolf's intention was to entertain the particularity of individual cultures and societies as they meshed with global dynamics, the impression remained that political economy was a macro perspective which invited library studies rather than field work. This probably explains why so few anthropologists have worked within the political economy tradition.

What is striking about the post-positivist era is that virtually all of the major theoretical orientations (the main exceptions being Lévi-Strauss's structuralism and Geertz's interpretive anthropology) and counter-discipline perspectives have placed power at the top, or close to the top, of the agenda. In feminist anthropology and postmodernism, the authority of the researcher/writer was challenged, and representations of "the Other" (women and natives) were dismissed as ideological props for the Western male's privilege. In cultural studies, class was analyzed alongside the trends of fashion and literature, and the focus swung to the embedded power relations and vested interests obfuscated by literary genres. In multicultural and ethnic studies, culture became a resource in the struggle for advantage. The big question is whether these several sources of the focus on power have enough in common to constitute a fourth model, or whether it is more appropriate to regard them as several quasi-models. If the current focus on power, which is unparalleled at any previous time in history, does deserve to be dignified as a distinctive approach, it could be labelled the liberating model, because its common feature is the struggle for equality. Equally debatable, as will be shown in the next chapter, is whether a fifth model has been carved out by Eric Wolf, one that counters the critique of culture by attempting to demonstrate that culture by definition implies power and power implies culture.[5]

CONTRIBUTION OF PHILOSOPHY, POLITICAL SCIENCE AND SOCIOLOGY

In their introduction to *African Political Systems*, Fortes and Evans-Pritchard dismissed the writings of political philosophers as of little use or scientific value to anthropology. Yet a generation later, Swartz, Turner and Tuden (1976; orig. 1966) remarked that in order to advance the study of comparative politics, it was time to integrate philosophy (and political science and sociology) into anthropology. In the pages that follow, most of my attention will be directed at issues and arguments associated with political science and sociology. But first I want to acknowledge, if only in passing, the importance of philosophy for the understanding of power.

Hobbes's *Leviathan* and Machiavelli's *The Prince* are probably never out of print. Less well-known, but highly relevant to a contemporary audience, is Bertrand Russell's *Power: A New Social Analysis* (1938). Even if we go back to classical Greek philosophy, we can find the seeds of political theory. Long before Machiavelli had asserted that might is right, Thrasymachus in Plato's *Republic* had said the same thing. As for Aristotle, not only was his analysis of politics empirically based and couched in "a well-defined analysis of social structure" (Weissleder 1978:188), but he also held the viewpoint, widespread in anthropology today, that politics is an aspect of all behavior and does not exist in isolation from other types of behavior or institutions. The one discipline in the social sciences that appears to have little to say about power is economics. This is curious, because surely economic goods and goals and the choices made to realize them are charged with power and politics. In this context, the words of Galbraith hit home (1983:xiii): "economics divorced from the consideration of power is without meaning and certainly without relevance."

STATE POWER

In this age of globalization, with multinational corporations flexing their muscles, we might be less inclined than our predecessors to be impressed by the seemingly enormous power of the nation-state or to regard its monopoly over power as impregnable. Yet it wasn't so long ago that Cohen (1978:1) wrote: "Give or take a few multinational corporations, the state is the most powerful organizational structure ever developed in the history of the planet." Perhaps the most influential definition of the state has been Weber's (1947:154–156): a compulsory political association that has a monopoly over the legitimate use of force within a given territory.

Although numerous anthropologists, from Radcliffe-Brown in his preface for *African Political Systems* to Bohannan in *Social Anthropology*, have embraced Weber's definition, this does not mean that fundamental changes in the nature of power since Weber's times have gone unrecognized. Mann (1993:315) distinguished between despotic power and infrastructural power. His argument was that in industrial societies the first type has declined greatly, while the second type has correspondingly increased. In fact, he contended, the power of the state in capitalist democracies has outstripped that of any previous stage in history, penetrating every aspect of human existence. Foucault, whose views on power we shall soon consider in some detail, suggested that the analysis of power has gone through three stages. The first focused on sovereign power, the power of kings. The second, dominated by the Marxists, dealt with state power. The third, liberated from the Marxists, emerged out of the turmoil of the student revolt that swept the streets of Paris in 1968, undermining the role of the revolutionary hero, and redirecting attention to the power-drenched discourses that inform just about every human relationship imaginable.[6]

Long before Foucault became an intellectual guru,[7] the Marxian perspective on the state and on power had been the subject of controversy. Marx argued (see Olsen and Marger 1993: 75) that power relations precede the state. They originate in economic production and are manifested in class structure. The state emerges simply to serve as an ideological support for the dominant class. In the non-Marxist or liberal perspective, a large degree of autonomy is attributed to the state. It is the state that generates power, reflected in governmental structure and the military machine; class struggle, rather than having a prior existence, grows out of state formation. In anthropology, Fried belongs to the Marxian camp, Service to the non-Marxist camp. Fried (1967) argues that the state props up the class system that preceded it, and portrays the world as one of conflict and division. Service (1975) describes the state not only as a hierarchical system with a monopoly over the use of force, but also as a fundamental source of societal integration; the state provides services and a sense of unity to its citizens, who in turn grant it legitimacy. In the end, the controversy between the Marxian and non-Marxian perspectives on the state boils down to yet another restatement of the perennial consensus–conflict controversy.

COMMUNITY POWER

Just as the literature on state power was dominated by a fundamental debate, the same was true for community power. The battle lines for the debate were laid down by two classical community studies in America, both produced by political scientists. One was Floyd Hunter's *Community Power Structure* (1953), the other Robert Dahl's *Who Governs?* (1961). Hunter's approach was called *reputational analysis*. Important figures in the community were first identified, and then judges were given the job of ranking them according to their influence. Hunter discovered a hierarchy of power dominated by businessmen. His conclusion was that elitism ruled the day. Dahl's approach was called *event analysis*. Rather than prejudging whether or not a community was stratified, a number of key issues currently being grappled with by members of the community were examined in order to determine how decisions were made, who made them, and who benefited. Dahl found that power was dispersed throughout the community, with no specific sector in control. His conclusion was that democratic pluralism prevailed.

Although Hunter's thesis was not rejected by everyone, and questions were raised about how Dahl decided what issues counted as key ones, the vast majority of commentators found the pluralist thesis more persuasive. The major criticism of Hunter was that his research design virtually made the conclusion inevitable that society was widely stratified, with a powerful elite at the top.

With Hunter out of the picture, the debate about elitism and pluralism mutated into one over agency and structure. Bachrach and Baratz (1962, 1963, 1970) argued that there are two faces of power: decisions and non-decisions. The pluralists, they stated, only focused on the first face. Yet the second was equally important and pervasive. Local councils, for example, ordered by federal law to terminate racial segregation in schools, could maintain the status quo simply by keeping the issue off the agenda. Both faces of power as portrayed by Bachrach and Baratz were intentional, reflecting human agency. However, they also entertained another type of power: structural power. Structural power flowed out of "the mobilization of bias" in society; that is, it reflected institutionalized advantage and disadvantage along the lines, for example, of class, gender and race. In the end, however, it was apparent that the authors only had flirted with structural power, for they reverted to a model in which the intentional decisions and non-decisions of individuals dominated the scene.

It was not long until Lukes (1974) introduced the three-dimensional model of power. Under the first dimension he included Dahl's pluralism and Bachrach and Baratz's decisions. Under the second dimension he placed non-decisions. Lukes' third dimension consisted of the sheer weight and shape of the institutional framework; in other words, it was structural power, the type identified but dropped by Bachrach and Baratz. Both the first and second dimension of power (decisions and non-decisions) were intentional, while the third (structural power) was unintentional. Of course we could rearrange this model to show that there were actually only two dimensions: intentional power (including decisions and non-decisions) and unintentional power (structural power).

Lukes' study was barely off the press when the major criticism against it was launched. The charge was that like his predecessors he had toyed with the notion of structural power only to discard it in favor of the deliberate exercise of power by individuals. As Bradshaw pointed out (1976:126): "Lukes himself came to argue that power lies ultimately in the *individual agents.*" In a brief and rather feeble reply, Lukes (1976) denied that he had given up on structural power, yet that was belied by his later essay on "Power and Structure" (1977), where he insisted that power belongs to agency. With all this in mind, Isaac's observation (1987:38) appears to be entirely justified: "In the end Lukes leans towards a view of power differing little from that of his predecessors in the debate."

At this juncture it would be easy to conclude that structural power isn't very important, or at least is beyond our capacity to conceptualize and analyze, especially if we want to include it alongside agency power. But then there is the work of Isaac. Drawing inspiration from Marx,[8] he attempts to demonstrate the significance of structural power, and he insists that if power is to be understood, structure and agency must be combined. In Isaac's words (1987:81): "the understanding of social structure I rely on rejects any bifurcation of structure and agency ... social power refers to the capacities to act possessed by agents by virtue of their social relations." In other words, individuals do deliberate and do make their own history, but always within the parameters set by social structure.

Stripped down to the bones, the debate about community power exposes some of the basic conceptual oppositions in the social sciences: hierarchy vs. equality (or elitism vs. pluralism, or closed vs. open systems), structure vs. agency (or unintentional vs. intentional), deductive vs. inductive, and conflict vs. consensus. In political science the weight of opinion was lined up behind the second side of these oppositions. The situation in anthropology would probably be more ambiguous, with some anthropologists swayed by agency and induction and others by hierarchy and conflict. What is clear is that there is considerable overlap between Dahl's pluralism and the transactional model in anthropology. In both cases room is made for the individual as innovator, and field work is the litmus test for investigating and explaining power, rather than a preconceived model.

One last observation: In most of the community studies produced by political scientists, as Bachrach and Baratz have pointed out, force and authority have been virtually ignored. Moreover, Weber's conception of power as the capacity of people to make others do things even against their wills has, as Spinrad (1966:221–222) made clear, been "generally irrelevant to most discussions of American community power." In view of all this, it is dubious whether anthropologists of the transactional persuasion would welcome any suggestion that they enjoy a cosy relationship with the pluralists.

INDIVIDUAL POWER

To the extent that pluralists like Dahl did participant observation research, they were in a favorable position to examine power at the individual or micro level, but this of course is where anthropologists have excelled. By individual power I do not mean psychological power, but instead that which is conditioned by the interaction of two or more persons. To illustrate power at the individual level, I shall provide some examples that deal with tactics, reputation, and ambition.[9]

1. Tactics of Power

We begin with the display of anger. A couple of years ago I took a group of Canadian students to Paris for a semester. The day after they had been installed in a residence, the director sent me a note stating that the students had gone wild, keeping everybody else awake all night; if their behavior did not immediately improve, she threatened, they would be tossed out on the street. When I attempted to meet with the director, I was informed by her assistant that she was too agitated even to discuss the matter with me. A few weeks later another contingent of foreign students arrived, and once again the director flew off the handle. The implication was clear. Feigned fury was her routine tactic of establishing quick control over the residents.

The opposite tactic, the display of good humor, can be equally effective. Canada's current prime minister, Jean Chrétien, is likely to counter concerns about high rates of unemployment or the plunging value of the dollar with words to the effect of "don't worry, be happy." When he was questioned about a volatile political confrontation in which pepper spray had been used to quell protesters, he joked that pepper is what he puts on his steak. In this context, humor trivializes what otherwise might transpire into a grave political threat.

Then there are what might be called the tranquillizing tactics. In northern Ontario some Aboriginal people who complained to the government received letters choked by jargonese, hardly an invitation to continue their inquiries. In Nigeria an acquaintance who required an official document, but refused to pay a bribe, was repeatedly asked to return on the pretext that the document was misplaced. Government reports addressed to social issues such as racism, sexism, and corruption often are part of the tranquillizing tactics, giving the false impression that something is being done. The chair of a university department with which I was once associated had an interesting method of dealing with sensitive issues and personality clashes. He simply ignored them, with the predictable result that most people eventually lost interest. As he explained to me, his goal was not to establish harmony, but merely to suppress open hostility. When the latter did occur, he turned to another tactic, inviting the parties involved to vent their anger on him, usually absorbing it before it reached epidemic proportions.

Of course, tactics of power also operate at the societal level. A nation-state, when crowded by another, may launch an attack, but even the threat of mobilization may be a sufficient deterrent. Ideology also plays its part. A ruling class may successfully persuade the masses that their interests coincide, or portray the status quo as natural or God's way. Then there is Gramsci's scheme in which force and consent reinforce hegemony, force only being resorted to infrequently because it carries a greater risk to the elite than does ideologically induced consent.

2. Power as Reputation

In human relations there seems to be a credit/debit ledger on reputation, with some people in the red and others in the black, regardless of their capabilities. In the first category we find the tainted individual. For example, in Nigeria I knew an elderly man appropriately nicknamed "Immortality." He had succumbed to repeated accusations of witchcraft, and thereafter was the first on the list when something went wrong in his community. Closer to home are colleagues in the university setting who get labelled as troublemakers, which often just means that they are too left-wing oriented for the administration. In my experience, there is virtually nothing these individuals can do to have the label removed, except by moving on to another institution. Those who remain react in one of two ways. Some simply accept the cards that have been dealt, and keep their heads low. Others do battle on a daily basis, spying a conspiracy around every corner. Their aggressive defensive reaction may be all that stands between them and defeat, but it also confirms their reputations as agitators.

In the second category is the individual with a halo. This is the type of person who can't seem to do anything untoward. Charges of wrongdoing can be made against the person, but they just won't stick. Doors will open even if competitors have greater, or at least equal, qualifications. Although behind the halo might be attributes such as the right family and religion, there also is a more nebulous element: charm. These are "feel good" people whose optimism is contagious. A couple of qualifications must be made. Sometimes "too affable" people, those who exude pleasantness and goodwill, are subjected to unfair treatment just because everyone knows they won't kick up a storm. Then there is the individual whose halo is rimmed with spikes, "the loose screw" type likely to throw a tantrum if thwarted. It is not charm that moves them up the ladder, although that may be the public face. Instead, it is the recognition that if the halo is dislodged, everyone else will suffer.

3. Degrees of Ambition

Some people seem to suffer from a deficit of ambition, others from an excess. In the first category we find the perfect lieutenant, the kind of person who no longer aspires to be top dog, if he or she ever did, being content to remain in the leader's shadow. In the village in West Africa where I conducted my Ph.D. research, such a person was the *oba*'s (king's) right-hand man. Although good humored and sociable, he was not considered by members of the community to be particularly capable. What he had going for him was a sunny disposition and absolute loyalty. The very idea that he would want to be the king would have struck people as preposterous. I would place Cheney, Bush's choice as vice-president in the U.S. election of 2000, in the same category—a reliable, loyal subaltern, who would not likely forget his place.

In the second category we find the imperfect lieutenant. This is the type of person near the top who wants it all. Often the tactic of the leader is to institutionalize the power of such competitors below his own. When the village in West Africa was founded, for example, the man who became *oba* had to deal with four aggressive competitors. He established an office called the four pillars, designating his rivals as deputy *obas*. Such institutionalization may curtail ambition, but it does not necessarily annihilate it. For example, Paul Martin, the finance minister in Chrétien's government, clearly occupied a formal position below that of the leader. Yet it was no secret that he wanted his boss's job. Indeed, some journalists argued that the main reason Chrétien called an early election in the fall of 2000 was to nip Martin's ambitions in the bud.

It would be easy to add to these examples of individual power, but I think that the point has been made. Power often operates in a way that deviates from normative and role expectations. This is most apparent at the level of the individual in interaction with others. Some transactionalists might interpret this conclusion to mean that the micro level, with its deviations, holds the key to understanding power and social life more generally. That is not my position. Individual power is merely a voice worth listening to, even when the noise coming from structural power is at its loudest.

THREE PIVOTAL FIGURES

Since World War II three theoreticians have significantly deepened our understanding of power. The first, C. Wright Mills, was a maverick sociologist who challenged the reigning consensus model and the academic establishment. The second, Talcott Parsons, in many respects *was* the sociological establishment. The third, Michel Foucault, has defied easy labelling. He has, much to his amusement, been called everything from Marxist to conservative, structuralist to anarchist, and anti-humanist to revolutionary hero.

1. C. Wright Mills

In two outstanding books, *White Collar* (1956; orig. 1951) and *The Power Elite* (1964; orig. 1956) Mills laid out the nuts and bolts of his argument. America, contrary to public opinion, is a class-based society dominated by a ruling class whose power possibly has been unrivalled anywhere in the world. The folk heroes of the past in America, the small businessman and the independent farmer, have been pushed aside by a power elite consisting of the leading figures in business, politics, and the military. The power elite's enormous control is not a result of a conspiracy on its part, but merely reflects its lofty class position. Not only do the top people in business, politics, and the military occupy "the command posts," but power itself has changed its shape since World War II. Legitimate power or authority, granted to leaders by the voluntarily obedient, has given way to manipulation. In other words, people do not even realize they are being moved around like pawns on a chessboard.

In addition to the power elite, two other classes exist. There is a middle level represented by Congress and most (ordinary) politicians, in which power is pluralistic, the manipulations of any single interest group balanced out by other groups. There also is a bottom level consisting of the unorganized, apathetic, bewildered masses. Even if they became aware of how they were being manipulated and decided to revolt, they wouldn't know who or what to attack, because power has become so vague and impersonal.

The reaction to Mills' analysis of American society was interesting for what it said about academia. Kolko (1971:222–223) enthusiastically embraced Mills, dismissing those who continued to describe America as an open, egalitarian society as naive apologists. Marvin Harris (1971:423), who also sided with Mills, noted that "there is much opposition, led by American sociologists and political scientists, to the notion that the United States has a 'ruling class.'" Harris was right on the mark about the opposition; most of the prominent sociologists at the time wrote Mills off as a nut case, or at least someone with socialist inclinations whose ideological commitment had distorted his scholarly objectivity.

Shortly after the publication of *White Collar*, David Reisman's *The Lonely Crowd* (1956) appeared. Reisman argued that there was no power elite in America. Instead, there were only two classes, a middle level and a lower level, corresponding to the second and third levels in Mills' scheme. Power in the middle level, according to Reisman, was pluralistic, with no single group in control. As for the lower level, rather than being manipulated and apathetic, the people there were willing allies of those who competed for power at the middle level, and shared in the benefits. In a comment on Reisman's pluralistic model of society in *The Power Elite* (1964:245), Mills recognizes that it does accurately describe the middle class, but has nothing to say about the elite that hovers over it.[10]

Mills (1964:9) embraced Weber's definition of power: "By the powerful we mean, of course, those who are able to realize their will, even if others resist it." It is precisely in relation to resistance that Mills has been especially vulnerable to attack. The contention of Kornhauser (1966) and others was that Mills ignored the constraints on the exercise of power. That is not the only aspect of Mills' conception of the elite that has been criticized. Like the renowned Italian elite theorists (Mosca, Pareto, and Michels), Mills has been accused of granting the power elite a life of its own, something that exists beyond the normal parameters of the class system, or the clash between capital and labor. While Mills might argue that this simply recognizes how America has changed, liberals would want to tie the elite to the state. Marxists, for their part, might think that it doesn't really matter who the elites are, since they are simply an expression of the relations of production, but the notion that they are autonomous and free-floating would strike them as ridiculous.

We now come to Mills' most vigorous, even vicious, critic: Talcott Parsons. In Parsons' view, Mills erroneously assumes that power is somehow illegitimate, overlooking its positive contribution. He also disagrees with virtually every important assertion made by Mills about American society, except the argument that the folk heroes of the past (the small businessman and independent farmer) have faded. Parsons scoffs at the idea of a power elite composed of the cream of the crop in business, politics, and the military, able to pull the wool over the faces of the unsuspecting majority.

Mills' arguments, of course, amounted to a massive repudiation of Parsonian consensus theory, [11] yet Parsons had almost always been gracious in replying to his critics.[12] Not so in the case of Mills. He criticized Mills' conception of power (a zero-sum game), his conception of the elite (describing it as a class), his empirical assertions (triumphant elites, defeated masses), and his scholarship (biased rather than value-neutral). It was Mills' personal politics, however, that really raised Parsons' ire (1960: 225): "It seems to me that he is clearly and ... unjustifiably anti-capitalist. He is partly pro-liberal and probably even more pro-socialist." Had Mills aimed his attack at the former Soviet Union, he might have been accepted along with Parsons as one of the grand figures in American sociology. But he had the gall to choose America as his target.

2. Talcott Parsons

Just as there were two faces of power at the community level (or three faces in Lukes' case), there were two faces of Parsons in terms of his analysis of power at the societal level. This is because he changed his mind in midstream about the nature of power and the status of political science.

In Parsons' original position set out in *The Social System* (1951), he followed Weber's zero-sum conception, and viewed power as a hierarchical relationship encompassing winners and losers. He also argued that political science was not a legitimate, independent discipline. One reason was that it did not possess an autonomous conceptual territory. In the Parsonian scheme, social action is the territory occupied by all the social sciences, its major divisions being the cultural system, the social system, and the personality system. Corresponding to these, and thus rendering them autonomous and legitimate, are the disciplines of anthropology, sociology, and psychology. Notably, there was no room within social action for political science, except as a subsystem of the social system. Another reason for denying political science the status of an independent discipline was the sheer diffuseness of power. Power, to draw upon one of Foucault's expressions, is "always-already" there. It is embedded throughout social action; one would have to entertain all the variables of the social system in order to begin to understand it. Parsons concluded that political science is at best a synthesizing discipline, not one with its own body of theory.

Parsons took quite a different position about economics, even though it too in his scheme was considered to be a subsystem of the social system. Economics, he thought, was a legitimate discipline because unlike political science it was concerned with a highly specific and distinctive problem within the theory of social action: rational decision-making and its consequences for exchange relations.

Political scientists must have breathed a sigh of relief when Parsons' revised position appeared in print. It turned out that they did, after all, possess a genuine and distinctive academic discipline; moreover, it had a lot in common with economics, mainly because power was said to operate somewhat similar to money. As Parsons put it (1966:243): "Power is here conceived as a circulating medium, analogous to money, within what is called the political system." His new position was explained even more clearly elsewhere (1960:181–182): "Parallel to the economy ... I believe that we can speak of a functional subsystem of the society in the political area, conveniently referred to as the 'polity'. The goal or function of the economy is *production* ... the product is income or wealth. The goal or function of the polity I conceive to be the mobilization of societal resources and their commitment for the attainment of *collective* goals, for the formation and implementation of 'public policy.' The 'product' of the polity as a system is *power*, which I would like to define as *the generalized capacity of a social system to get things done in the interest of collective goals.*"

Parsons had fundamentally changed his mind about the nature of power. Power no longer was a relationship but rather a system property. It did not involve hierarchy but instead the distribution of collective benefits. Force had no connection to it because power was totally legitimate. This last point needs some explanation. Whereas most writers prior to Parsons separated power and authority, and viewed the latter as a special case of the former (power that had been institutionalized), he reversed the equation. That is, authority preceded power, providing the latter with the legitimacy it required. As Giddens observed, Parsons came to see authority not as a type of power but instead as the basis for power.

For writers like Mills who regarded force as the final or most fundamental form of power, Parsons' argument must have been difficult to swallow. Yet Parsons did not lack admirers. The anthropologists Swartz, Turner, and Tuden (1976:14; orig. 1966) referred to his emphasis on the legitimacy of power as "stimulating." And as both Habermas (1986) and Wrong (1979) pointed out, Arendt's conception of power was very similar to Parsons'. She too (1986) divorced force from power, and viewed power as positive and legitimate, oriented to the attainment of collective goals. Much more critical of Parsons' change of heart was Anthony Giddens. Pointing out that what it achieved was to bring his treatment of power in line with the consensus position in *The Social System*, Giddens observed (1968:268): "Parsons' account of power and the electoral process reads like a description of normative democratic theory in general, and often like an *apologia* for American democracy in general." In this context we might well reflect on Keesing's comment about the contribution of legitimacy to the dominant class (1976:364): "The very legitimacy of its authority is an ideology created by the politically powerful and imposed on the powerless: the notion of consent becomes meaningless. Legitimacy is not a societal contract, but an instrument of power."

To sum up, my own viewpoint is that Mills has been a much better prophet than Parsons in understanding the world we live in. When the financial clout necessary to stand as a presidential candidate in America is considered, along with the low voter turnout, images of power elites and apathetic masses are difficult to avoid. Yet what seemed to worry most people about the post-election battle in the year 2000 between Bush and Gore was whether the ultimate victor would have sufficient legitimacy to effectively govern the nation. The implication is that Parsons was dead on the mark in arguing that legitimacy is a critical dimension of power. Whether it is the masses or the elite who benefit from it is quite another matter.

3. Michel Foucault

Every now and then a scholar emerges with a message that is so profound and novel, or tantalizingly complex, that it attracts the attention of people across the academic community. Michel Foucault, like Marx and Lévi-Strauss before him, was precisely this rare breed of scholar. His perspective, referred to by Digeser (1992) as the fourth face of power, was set out in his studies of prisons, mental institutions, sexuality, and the relationship between power and knowledge. It was also clarified in a number of charming interviews in which he emerged as a humane and modest individual.

Foucault is not easy to understand, and the reasons are more than the Parsonian-like jargon and the novelty and profundity of his ideas. There also is a considerable amount of inconsistency and contradiction in his writings. His reputation is that of a theorist of power, and indeed he has acknowledged (1988:101–102) that when he began to investigate madness and prison life there was one question that seemed to be at the center of everything: what is power? Yet he has stated (1988:39): "I am far from being a theoretician of power. At the limit, I would say that power, as an autonomous question, does not interest me." Elsewhere he has remarked (1984:385) that he has "never tried to analyze anything whatsoever from the point of view of politics." In *The History of Sexuality* (1978:82) he tells us that it is an "analytics" of power, not a theory of power, that he has attempted to construct.

Occasionally Foucault complained that his readers had failed to understand his arguments. For example, after *Les Mots et les Choses* was published, he was referred to as a philosopher who promoted intellectual discontinuity. Yet his purpose, he explained (1988:100), was precisely the opposite: to examine discontinuity as a problem, and attempt to resolve it. Similarly, he has been heralded for identifying knowledge with power. His response was one of ridicule (1988:43):

"when I read ... the thesis, 'Knowledge is power,' or 'Power is knowledge,' I begin to laugh, since studying their *relation* is precisely my problem. If they were identical, I would not have to study them and I would be spared a lot of fatigue as a result." In this context, he has pointed out that in his work on hospitals he found that the same form of power can generate different forms of knowledge. He also cautioned us not to accept the common notion that power and knowledge are inversely related; that is, knowledge only becomes possible when power is suspended or destroyed. His counter argument is that power can not only stifle knowledge but also encourage it.

It is easier to understand what power is not, in Foucault's perspective, rather than what it is.[13] Power is not a substance, structure, institution, or personality characteristic. It "is not something that is acquired, seized, or shared, something that one holds onto or allows to slip away"(1978:94). It is not an ideological mechanism that assures the subservience of the masses. It is not primarily a system of domination at the societal level. Nor are relations of power in any way separate from sexual, economic, knowledge, or any other types of relationships.

Foucault locates power at the micro level of behavior. In his words (1988:83): "Power is only a certain type of relation between individuals." Elsewhere (1978:93) we read: "it is the name that one attributes to a complex strategical situation in a given society." And again (1978:94): "Power comes from below; that is, there is no binary and all-encompassing opposition between rulers and ruled at the root of power relations." Power, he states (1978:93), "is the moving substrate of force relations."

To understand what Foucault means by *power*, it is necessary to relinquish the neat and tidy world of positivism, with independent and dependent variables and logical cause and effect. In Foucault's epistemology, everything seems to be happening at once. Power suppresses an activity, then encourages it. Power is the cause of something that happens, but also its effect. Power opposes knowledge while simultaneously nourishing it. Power is ever on the move, generating coalitions and then disrupting them, settling momentarily on individuals and then flitting through institutions, leaving both individual and institution ravished or enriched in the process. Power is both positive and negative, intentional and unintentional. In Foucault's famous expression, power is always-already there—another sort of uninvited guest, à la Lévi-Strauss, whose significance we cannot ignore.

This complex, dynamic, topsy-turvy conception of power permeates two of the topics on which his fame rests: discourse and resistance. Fontana and Pasquino (Foucault 1984:57) credit him as being the first person to analyze discourse in terms of power. This was the thrust of his work on sexuality. Rather than finding that discussion of sexuality was gradually repressed as industrialization occurred, interest in and concern about sexuality resulted in a greatly expanded discourse. It is in discourse, Foucault argued, that knowledge and power come together. But there isn't a dominant discourse and a subservient discourse, or a legitimate and illegitimate discourse. Instead there is "a multiplicity of discursive elements" that criss-cross the social fabric. In Foucault's words (1978:100–101): "We must make allowances for the complex and unstable process whereby discourse can be both an instrument and an effect of power, but also a hindrance, a stumbling block, a point of resistance and a starting point for an opposing strategy. Discourse transmits and produces power; it reinforces it, but also undermines and exposes it, renders it fragile and makes it possible to thwart it."

This last comment leads directly to the topic of resistance, and to what is perhaps his most famous message: where there is power there is resistance. Although some critics such as Sangren (1995) have interpreted this to mean that resistance exists apart from power, that is not what Foucault meant (1988:123): "I am not positing a substance of resistance versus a substance of power. I am just saying: as soon as there is a power relation there is a possibility of resistance." Indeed, he argues (1988:83–84) that if such possibility does not exist, then force rather than power is involved.

Just as there are a multitude of discourses, rather than grand binary ones reflecting structured advantage and disadvantage, there are a multitude of resistances. Foucault allows that occasionally these various points of resistance can converge, producing social cleavages and revolutionary action, but that is unusual. As he states (1978:96): "more often one is dealing with mobile and transitory points of resistance, producing cleavages in society that shift about, fracturing unities and effecting regroupings, furrowing across individuals themselves, cutting them up and remolding them.... Just as the network of power relations ends by forming a dense web that passes through apparatuses and institutions, without being localized in them, so too the swarm of points of resistance traverses social stratifications and individual unities."

Original and influential Foucault's approach to power undoubtedly has been, but it has not escaped criticism. Sangren (1995) has commented on the remarkable similarity between power and resistance in Foucault's work and yin and yang in Chinese conceptions of power, dismissing both conceptions as ideological and metaphysical. Then, too, it is interesting to note that in divorcing force from power, Foucault has lined himself up alongside Parsons and Arendt. Parsons' early view of power is so diffused that analysis of it is rendered futile, and even his revised image in which power moves back and forth across the polity comparable to the manner in which money traverses the economy, resonate with Foucault's description. Marxists who want to embrace Foucault as one of their own, despite his declaration that he is neither pro nor anti Marx, can take no pleasure from the common ground that he shares with Parsons; or from his expressed disinterest in ideology as a form of power.[14] As for Weberians, and anthropologists aligned with the transactional school of politics, Foucault's take on human agency must have turned their stomachs. Foucault certainly did concentrate on the micro level of human interaction. Yet he denied human agency or subjectivity (Sangren 1995), adopted an extreme anti-humanist and anti-structuralist position (Gane 1986), and treated individuals as mere "bodies" occupying statistical space (Wickham 1986).

This last point brings us to yet another novel concept introduced by Foucault: bio-power. His argument was that in the eighteenth century scientific categories such as species, fertility, and birth and death rates became politicized; that is, governments began to appreciate the importance of controlling their populations. At the same time the body, under the influence of what Foucault referred to as "disciplinary technology," became an object to be molded, manipulated and rendered malleable and docile for the benefit of the state and its institutions. Such was the significance of bio-power that Foucault (1978:140–141) claimed it to be "an indispensable element in the development of capitalism."

If we take a step back in order to catch the writings of Mills, Parsons, and Foucault at one glance, certain patterns emerge. Mills' approach to power is clear but not complex, guided by a conventional (positivistic) epistemology, and favoring the conflict model of society; its claim to novelty is based on the characterization of America as a class-organized society dominated by the elite. Parsons' approach is complex but not clear, with a conventional epistemology and a consensus orientation; generally speaking, Parsons is a synthesizer rather than a novel theoretician, although his revised conception of power as positive, legitimate, and oriented to the collective good represents a clean break from Weber. Foucault's approach is complex and not clear, and his epistemology is certainly novel; whether he should be described as a conflict or consensus theoretician is an open question, since evidence for both positions exists in his writings. Beyond any doubt his conception of power is innovative, and his contribution to our understanding of discourse and resistance important. Whether these ideas will endure is another matter. As we shall next see, already there are signs that discourse and resistance have begun to feel their ages.

DISCOURSE

Foucault's analysis of discourse apparently inspired Said's impressive study, *Orientalism*, which in itself was no mean feat. However, there has been a backlash against the textual analysis associated with discourse. The argument is not necessarily that discourse is irrelevant, but rather that there is more to power and oppression than the text. Parkin (1990:183) suggests that the time has come to separate literary critique from actual political and military policies and power. Pointing out that differences generated by power relations exist prior to and independent from the manner in which they are represented, Gupta and Ferguson (1992:17) state: "there is thus a politics of otherness that is not reducible to a politics of representation. Textual strategies can call attention to the politics of representation, but the issue of otherness itself is not really addressed by the devices of polyphonic textual construction or collaboration with informant-writers, as writers like Clifford and Craganzano seem to suggest." Gupta and Ferguson aren't in favor of scrapping the emphasis on textual representation; but they do argue that it must be complemented by examining power beyond the parameters of the text.

A somewhat similar position has been adopted by Abu-Lughod. As she points out (1991:143), the postmodern venture, with the emphasis on dialogic or polyvocal texts, as well as earlier efforts by anthropologists to come to grips with racism and colonialism, have failed to dent global power relations. It should be added that Clifford himself, in his preface to *Writing Culture*, frankly admitted that a textual analysis can't fully cope with institutionalized inequality and global domination.

Other problems connected to postmodern textual analysis have been recognized, such as the fact that regardless of the effort to be dialogic, and to think in terms of collaborators and consultants rather than informants, the author retains control over the final product. Not even Clifford's writings, as Rabinow pointed out (1986), are dialogic. Clifford would readily concur, having earlier (1983:140) referred to plural authorship as an unattainable utopia. Then there is the irksome problem of the reader's interpretation. Even writers with the least misanthropic intentions may find that they have failed to negotiate the politics of writing ethnography. For example, a schoolteacher in Ireland, unhappy with Scheper-Hughes' *Saints, Scholars and Schizophrenics* (1982), complained (see Brettel 1992:13): "It's not your science I'm questioning, but this: don't we have the right to lead unexamined lives, the right *not* to be analyzed?" Ironically, what upset some people was that Scheper-Hughes had written a book that was so easy for them to read.

RESISTANCE

When I was conducting my first sustained field work project a long time ago in a small community along the coastal swamps of Nigeria, I became friendly with a middle-aged man from the mainland who came to visit his niece every couple of months. She had been hired by the community as a nurse, but caught the eye of the *oba*, who persuaded her to become one of his wives. Her uncle confided in me that he was displeased with the turn of events. Yet in the company of the *oba* he was respectful to the point of being obsequious—a gentle, delicate man, I thought, perhaps even a weak one.

As he prepared to return to the mainland during one of his visits, I asked if I could travel with him, hoping he would give me a ride in his car and perhaps even put me up for the night in his house. I was mildly surprised, in view of our amicable relationship, when he expressed some reluctance; but my reaction then was nothing compared to what I felt after we arrived at his compound. This apparently docile, timid human being turned into a tiger. Bristling with authority, he mobilized his daunted wives, children, and servants, and soon corners were being cleaned and cooking pots were bubbling. His attitude towards me was similarly transformed. Lofty Ph.D. candidate from a faraway land I might be, but on his territory I was a minor figure to be temporarily tolerated, as long as I knew who was boss.

This seems to be a good example of how people resist; they conceal part of themselves. That was also the tactic used by a man whom I met in Sudan. I arrived in his country ragged and soiled, after hitchhiking from Nigeria across the center of Africa. He was introduced to me by some American businessmen. From their perspective, he was a most genial and loyal employee, and when they asked him to serve as my guide for a couple of days, he graciously accepted the assignment. Where we went was to the Red Sea, fishing rods in hand. Cramped into a tiny boat, more a captive than a companion, I soon was made aware of another side of the man. It turned out that he was a committed Marxist, well-read, articulate, and fueled with nationalistic fervor. He despised the Americans, and his attitude towards me was not very different. What, he repeatedly asked, had I done to the "red Indians" of Canada?

Resistance, thanks to Foucault, and to scholars such as Scott (1985), has become a sexy topic in anthropology, an opportunity to side with the underdog and celebrate its capacity to fight back. A sober second look, however, has dampened some of the early enthusiasm. One argument has been that the emphasis on resistance is tantamount to recognizing that large-scale rebellion and revolutionary change are luxuries of the past. All that is left is resistance, and its impact on power relations is minimal. Ortner (1995) has put her finger on another weak spot. Resistance has been romanticized. It has been interpreted as testimony to the human craving for dignity and freedom, evidence that the human spirit is indomitable. While Ortner criticizes existing studies of resistance for being ethnographically thin, and for overlooking internal dissension among resisters, she still thinks it is an important concept because it evokes power in human relationships. Quite a different position has been adopted by Brown (1996). Sarcastically referring to resistance as the perfect vehicle for moral fervor because it doesn't really mean anything, he expresses considerable regret about the current prominence of both resistance and power in anthropology, which he attributes to the unfortunate influence of Foucault and feminist studies. Whatever happened, he asks, to the other side of the picture: cooperation, reciprocity, altruism, and the creative power of the imagination?

Perhaps the most intriguing second look at resistance has been taken by Abu-Lughod (1990). She too refers to resistance as a romanticized form of small-scale subversions, the subject of interest because large-scale collective resurrections have become increasingly improbable. But she does something more. Rather than following Foucault's famous formula, "where there is power there is resistance," she turns it around, so that it becomes "where there is resistance there is power." As Abu-Lughod concluded, this swings the balance away from resistance as a romantic phenomenon and towards the strategies and structures of power that give rise to it.[15]

CONCLUSION

Around 1970, when I was a graduate student in England, I came across a research proposal written by the eminent scholar, Edmund Leach. It apparently had been distributed to anthropology departments across the country. Along with the proposal, if I recall correctly, were the laudatory evaluations of the referees selected by the funding agency to which the proposal had been submitted. The proposal, intended as a model for neophyte scholars, was indeed well-crafted. Yet it also amounted to a lovely display of the authority and influence of the social anthropological establishment. I have sometimes wondered whether Leach, the man who had pointed to power as possibly the most basic human motive, extracted a bit of wry humor from the situation, or instead merely accepted it as his due. Whichever the case, this example illustrates one of the repeated messages in the literature: power is everywhere; nothing that is fashioned by humans can avoid it.

Another lesson is that for those who aspire to value-neutrality, there can be hardly anything more challenging than the study of politics and power. Consider the ease by which various models can be reduced to either conflict or consensus. This raises another issue. Some anthropologists, perhaps especially those with applied interests, seem to think that theory is largely irrelevant. Yet all of our research, applied or otherwise, has theory embedded in it, and the character of that theory is important. Reflect, for a moment, on the difference made by seeing the world through the lens of Mills opposed to Parsons, the structuralists rather than the transactionalists, or the community elitists instead of the pluralists. Occasionally even those scholars who feel more comfortable spouting theories or sitting in a library come down to ground level. Mills, for example (Horowitz 1967:7), was highly critical of people who treated the academy as a refuge, a place to shut out the cares of the world. Even Talcott Parsons, the self-designated incurable theorist, was not above producing applied work. Few scholarly articles could make a greater claim to the applied label than those he produced on Fascism and post-World War II reconstruction in Germany, notably "The Problem of Controlled Institutional Change" (1964; orig. 1945). Surprisingly, in view of his reputation as a revolutionary figure, it is Foucault who falls short when it comes to applied work. Remember his distinction between the universal and the specific intellectual. His argument was that the academic's role was not that of the pied piper; it was merely to decode the world so that people could better understand it and decide for themselves what to do, if anything. In other words, Foucault's position differed little from what many of us have long advocated: critical anthropology.

Much of the literature which has been reviewed deals with political structure and political activity, and its subtypes such as factions and decision-making, rather than power per se. When power is zeroed in on, often it is via its aspects such as influence, manipulation, authority and force. In my judgment, this is all to the good. Power is at times too general and crude to be of much explanatory value on its own. This is especially the case when blatant conflict is involved. In that situation conflict and power are much the same thing. As several writers have suggested (Dahl 1963:73, Etzioni 1993:22, Nicholas 1976:52, Swartz et al. 1976:2), power and conflict are almost identical twins. When conflict is spotted, power can't be far away, and the converse. The analysis of conflict is tantamount to the analysis of power. What this means is that when we investigate situations of overt conflict and attempt to analyze them in terms of power, without turning to more nuanced concept, we essentially are engaged in a redundant exercise. Only when conflict is subtle and covert, or where harmony apparently prevails, does the mere mention of power possibly throw a fresh light on the subject.

In a somewhat similar fashion, it could be said that the attempt to erect an abstract analysis of power lacks purpose. Power cannot be found in the abstract. Ubiquitous it certainly is, but it only exists in the context of interaction and institutions. This is why Foucault, I think, preferred an analytics rather than a theory of power, and expressed disinterest in power as an abstraction. For anthropologists, this should be good news. Even if power remains at the top of the agenda, we can accommodate it by going about our business as usual: probing social action and structure, poking into the informal pockets of everyday life.

NOTES

1. This line of analysis set the stage for the conflict model articulated by Gluckman (1956), who was one of the contributors to *African Political Systems*.

2. Of course, the publication coincided with the outbreak of World War II, which found most British anthropologists involved in war service of one kind or another. To be more precise, then, it was probably not until the late 1940s that the excitement peaked.

3. P.C. Lloyd has been credited (Kurtz 1979:35) with elevating decision-making to a central position in political anthropology. By a stroke of luck rather than rational design, I studied in England under two of the leading political anthropologists of the times: Lloyd and Bailey.

4. It should be pointed out, however, that M.G. Smith was one of the few anthropologists around at the time who had a sound grasp of Weber's work, as reflected in his analysis of pre-industrial stratification systems (Smith 1966).

5. Kurtz (2001) contends that there have been five main paradigms in political anthropology: functionalism, processual, political economy, political evolution, and postmodernism.

6. By accident, I was in Paris at that time, and much to my discredit hardly had a clue about what was going on.

7. This certainly is ironical, since he argued that the universal intellectual had been replaced by the specific intellectual, which simply meant that academics no longer led the masses by virtue of the special "truth" they possessed.

8. Isaac (1987:144), incidentally, sharply disagrees with those critics who contend that Marx did not have a theory of power: "Marx's theory of capitalist production is a theory of power; and his theory of power is a theory of capitalist production."

9. While my approach will be ethnographic, it should be pointed out that there is a highly rigorous brand of microsociology among sociologists concerned with the individual, one moreover that deals with power. See Collins (1981) and MacKinnon (1994).

10. It might be thought that Hunter's elitist model supports Mills' position, and Dahl's pluralism reinforces Reisman's. However, as Spinrad (1966) argued, it is not legitimate

to generalize from the community level to the societal level. Mills himself, in reference to Warner's community studies, said exactly the same thing.

11. See his trivialization of Parsonian sociology in *The Sociological Imagination* (1959).

12. See, for example, his response to (the mostly friendly) critics in Black (1961).

13. For one of his most explicit statements on power, see the *History of Sexuality*, Vol. 1, pp. 92–102, 1978.

14. Although he apparently was a member of the French Communist Party in his youth (Gane 1986:6), he has stated (1980:58): "As regards Marxism, I'm not one of those who try to elicit the effects of power at the level of ideology."

15. Foucault himself (see 1982:209–211), as Abu-Lughod pointed out, alluded to a similar inversion, which transformed resistance into "a chemical catalyst" that identified power relations and their structures and strategies.

Chapter 3

Power, Culture, and Social Structure

Although Abu-Lughod and company scored a direct hit on the culture concept, contending that difference was exaggerated and inequality ingrained, it wasn't the only shot fired. In recent years even Culture (with a large C), supposedly the defining feature of Homo sapiens, has occasionally come under attack. Both Murphy (1971:48–49) and Moore (1974), for example, have argued that other species such as chimpanzees and macaques are capable of learned and transmitted behavior, and thus have Culture.[1] More surprisingly still, cultural relativism, the moral and epistemological core of the discipline, has been challenged. As Yengoyan has observed (1986:371), hardly any other social science accepts cultural relativism, which is dismissed "as a game that pervades anthropology as a means of maintaining cultural differences." According to philosophers such as Jarvie (1983), who envisage universal principles of morality and truth, relativism unavoidably degenerates into nihilism. Within anthropology itself, the onslaught against relativism has been considerable. Bennett (1987:50) suggests that it became a bankrupt position in the wake of the Nazi regime, and argues that culture sometimes is a "divisive and destructive force in human affairs."

Several years ago Edgerton (1978) asserted that not just individuals but entire societies may be deviant and inadequate. More recently he has pointed out (1999) that some of our leading figures such as Linton, Kroeber, and Redfield rejected relativism, arguing that not all cultures are equal, that not all aspects of culture are adaptable or functional, and that there are universal standards that mark complex, "civilized" societies as superior. The notion of superior societies is certainly controversial, and in fairness to Edgerton it should be indicated that in his judgment maladaptive beliefs and practices are found in all societies, not just folk ones.[2]

Jacques Parizeau, a former leader of the secessionist-inclined Parti Québécois, recently remarked that English Canada did not possess a genuine culture; instead, its "culture" was a crass invention of the ruling Liberal Party. This brings us in sight of another potential blow to the cultural concept: the discovery that "tradition" is often invented, with anthropologists sometimes doing the inventing. Indeed, primitive society, according to Kuper (1988), is nothing more than an illusion created by anthropologists in order to enhance preconceived theoretical positions. Yet not everyone is disturbed by the news that traditions are often invented. As Hobsbawm (1983:4) points out, that is a normal process in all societies, especially during periods of rapid social change, when continuity with the past is threatened.[3] According to Hanson (1990) two traditions that have enjoyed widespread acceptance by the Maori regarding their origins were actually conceived by European scholars committed to the view that Maori and European culture were similar, and bound to converge in the future. While Hanson cautions that this does not make them unauthentic, the very idea of an invented tradition is politically explosive. Hanson's article, for example, was latched onto by elements of the New Zealand media as evidence that current Maori aspirations for independence, or autonomy, may not be entirely legitimate.

It was in this context, with culture under attack from all directions, that several anthropologists began to fight back. Most of them gave the impression that it was a matter of culture *or* power, but Eric Wolf thought in terms of culture *and* power. The way to revitalize culture, he thought, was to hook it up to power.

WRITING FOR CULTURE AGAIN: CULTURE OR POWER

Although by the 1990s the culture concept's obituary had already been composed, some anthropologists claimed it was a case of mistaken identity. This is because, in their viewpoint, the image of culture held by its critics bore little resemblance to the real thing. That image, according to Brightman (1995), attributed a number of properties to culture such as holism, localism, coherence, homogeneity, primordialism, idealism, discreteness, and ahistoricism. Yet arguably just as prominent have been agency, strategy, heterogeneity, fragmentation, and historical change. Brightman accuses the critics of culture of being guilty of disciplinary amnesia, either because they are ignorant of how culture has been defined in the past, or because they have intentionally distorted the record. With the latter in mind, Brightman (1995:527) dismisses the image of culture held by the critics as concocted "inventions," the product of "selective forays into disciplinary history," and observes: "When we encounter arguments today that the culture construct should be abandoned, we must naturally wonder which of its formulations from among all the possible ones we should be rid of."

In a bold and stimulating article in which the author's dismay at what has happened to anthropology simmers barely below the surface, Lewis picks up where Brightman finished, accusing the critics of distorting the diverse nature of culture and misrepresenting the discipline's accomplishments. Referring to the current "obsession with power and domination" (1998:717), he suggests that we started to get off track in the 1960s, when Marxism came in vogue, and have been completely derailed since then by postmodernism, literary theory, and cultural studies. What is lamentable, in his judgment, is that for the past quarter of a century or so the education of students has consisted of the critical attacks on the discipline, as if these represented the works of the past. In Lewis's words (p.717): "A terrible gap has opened up—an awesome chasm, in fact—separating this generation of students and younger anthropologists from the knowledge, data, theories, and understandings developed in the field up to about 1965."

Lewis fingers Keesing as one of the major culprits, especially his arguments (1994) that anthropology has treated people as "radically other," that the discipline has been ahistorical, and that each culture has been portrayed as an isolated unit. Anthropology, Lewis counters, was from its inception guided by the uniformitarian thrust of the Enlightenment; and cross-cultural similarities, not just differences, have always been the focus of the discipline. Observing just how much things have changed, he states (p.721): "One must now be embarrassed to take an interest in, let alone devote one's life to the study of, some group of people who are not immediately evident as one's own." While some of us might wonder why he overlooked the argument that culture emerged as a counter-Enlightenment concept (Geertz 1973:35, Wolf 1999:64), his dismissal of the ahistorical charge is much less controversial. After all, history was at the heart not only of evolutionism but also of the Boasian school. Nor do the Boasians, with their focus on diffusion, fit the image of culture as an isolated unit.

Summing up his displeasure with the critics of the culture concept, Lewis levels his own charge (p. 726): "The followers of Foucault, Edward Said, and Johannes Fabian have managed to do to anthropology what Said says Westerners have done to the Orient or to the Other: invent something that never existed in order to dominate it. Their version of anthropology—their invented anthropology—has served to 'otherize' and marginalize anthropologists and anthropological knowledge."

Unlike Lewis, Brumann (1999) does not ridicule the critique of culture mounted by Abu-Lughod, Keesing, and others, but he does argue that with some modifications the concept can and should be salvaged. While appreciating that consensus about beliefs and behavior within a culture is never total, he nevertheless suggests that it is sufficient to mark one culture off from another. Brumann also thinks that the acceptance of the concept beyond academia is a good reason for retaining it. Lay people, he points out (p. 12), have got at least part of the picture right: "culture is there, it is learned, it permeates all of everyday life, it is important, and it is far more responsible for differences among human groups than genes." In his reply to comments on the paper, Brumann (p. 23) introduces a novel suggestion: "when explaining the phenomena we are studying, we should start from the null hypothesis that they are not culturally caused and resort to culture only after explanations on the basis of the individual and the universal have failed." Treating culture as a residual category certainly recognizes its limits and makes room for other variables such as class and power. Yet one wonders why culture deserves this fate any more than any other variable, at least if it remains as serviceable as Brumann suggests.

Brightman, Brumann, and Lewis all complained that recent critics have ignored the remarkable diversity of the culture concept. They have a case. Culture is said to exist independent of our knowledge of it (realism), or only by virtue of such knowledge (idealism). For some writers it consists of symbols and rules and learned and shared behavior, for others just symbols and rules or just learned and shared behavior. Culture has been defined as an abstraction or logical construct, devoid of causal properties; it also has been touted as the master concept and dominant cause of almost everything in human life. Some writers such as Kroeber and White regarded culture as a reality *sui generis*, which explained itself, much like social facts in Durkheim's anti-reductionist perspective. In this sense, culture exists independent of individuals; yet in Goodenough's opinion (1994:267), it is precisely this rendition that lands the concept in hot water. Culture is said to be characterized by shared agreement and integration, or to vary from one individual to the next. In early American anthropology, Kroeber's superorganic expressed the first position, while Sapir emphasized intra-cultural variability (Darnell 1997), and Boas cautioned that integration could never be assumed. More recently, Vayda (1994:323) has adopted an extreme anti-essentialist view of culture, arguing that it is uniquely created by each individual. Probably the majority view today, following Wallace (1970), is that culture consists of the organization of diversity rather than the replication of uniformity.

Disagreement over the relationship between culture and social structure (or society) has been equally widespread, although this often reflects the vested interests of the American and British schools. Kroeber, who viewed culture and social structure as two sides of the same coin, thought that culture "rested" on and was "carried" by social structure. He also assumed that culture was the more critical variable because while other species have societies, only humans have culture. For Goody (1994), representing the British tradition, culture was merely an aspect of social structure, not the explanatory monolith sometimes portrayed in American anthropology. Verdon (1998:69 and 187), like Goody a Cambridge product, put the case against culture even more forcibly: culture amounts to little more than rationalization for existing patterns of behavior or social practices, its only causal prowess being a brake on subsequent change. According to Maxwell (1999:153), social structure is evidence of culture, but not the real thing; from Radcliffe-Brown's perspective the real thing *is* social structure, culture a fairy tale. Ironically, Gamst and Norbeck (1976:97) have suggested that Radcliffe-Brown's concepts of structure and function actually were synonyms for culture, and White (1976:64) claimed that Durkheim's social facts were culture traits. Little wonder that Robert Murphy (1971) quipped that in most ethnographies it wouldn't matter one iota which concept was used.

To sum up, it is apparent that culture has been defined in a remarkable variety of ways.[4] Whether this is regarded as an asset or liability is very much in the eye of the beholder. The champions of the culture concept are dazzled by its richness and flexibility. The critics see little except contradiction and confusion, and wonder about the sanity of its supporters.

Before turning to Wolf's work, it should be made clear that several other prominent scholars have come to the rescue of the culture concept. Lévi-Strauss (1994:424–425) has written: "Who can deny that, even taking internal differences into account, there is a Japanese culture, an American culture? There is no country more the product of a mixture than the United States, and nonetheless there exists an 'American way of life' that all inhabitants of the country are attached to, no matter what their ethnic origin." While arguing that the concept of culture must be cut down in size, D'Andrade (1999:100) has concluded: "Viewed not as everything, but as an important force in its own right, the concept of culture will continue to be indispensable." According to Goodenough (1994:263), even if the concept is ditched, we shall still have to find a way of conceptualizing and analyzing what it has stood for. His argument is that internal complexity notwithstanding, people sharing a geographical territory speak, play, and carry themselves differently than others. Then there is the surprising comment of Abu-Lughod (1999:14) in her reaction to Brumann's paper. Although she sticks to her guns regarding the demise of the culture construct, she states: "We all know in some sort of rough way that different groups of people share certain things, ways of thinking and doing. Who would deny it? And what other name is there for this?"

If we go back a little further in time and venture beyond the discipline, we find what were meant to be the encouraging words of Talcott Parsons. In the field of action, the social system was claimed by sociology and the personality system by psychology. That left the cultural system adrift. To the rescue came anthropology, thus completing the conceptual territory of the social sciences. Parsons (1951:545–555) contended that if anthropology was defined as the study of humankind, it was not an autonomous discipline, only a synthesizing one. Likewise, if it was seen as the study of social systems with a specialized focus on nonliterate societies (Parsons 1964:23–27), it was merely a branch of sociology. Only by becoming the discipline that specialized in culture could it claim the same autonomy and legitimacy enjoyed by sociology and psychology.

According to Geertz (1973:249–250) anthropologists are indebted to Parsons for another reason. Parsons pointed out that it doesn't help much to argue that people behave in a certain way because of their culture while defining culture as the way people behave. By excluding behavior from culture, Parsons made it logically possible to explain the first by the second without being tautological.

Geertz himself, of course, has been perhaps the most innovative thinker about the nature of culture since World War II. Culture, he states (1973:14), "is not a power, something to which social events, behaviors, institutions, or processes can be causally attributed; it is a context, something within which they can be intelligibly—that is, thickly—described." Aligning himself with a semiotic approach he remarks (1973:44): "culture is best seen not as complexes of concrete behavior patterns—customs, usages, traditions, habit clusters—as has, by and large, been the case up to now, but as a set of control mechanisms—plans, recipes, rules, instructions (what computer engineers call 'programs')—for the governing of behaviour." By conceiving culture as a literary text in need of interpretation, promoting generalization within cases (thick description) rather than across them, and characterizing cultures as incommensurate (epistemological relativism), Geertz may not have pleased everyone, but about his commitment to the culture construct there can be no doubt.[5]

CULTURE AND POWER

In *Envisioning Power: Ideologies of Dominance and Crisis* (1999), one of anthropology's most renowned practitioners, the late Eric R. Wolf, attempts to salvage culture by wedding it to power. Like most contemporary writers, he dismisses the conception of power as a substance or force, and suggests that we regard power as an aspect of all human relations. Echoing an earlier argument (1990), Wolf distinguishes between four modalities of power (p.5):

1. Power inherent in an individual (Nietzschean view).
2. Power as capacity of ego to impose her or his will on alter (Weberian view).
3. Power as control over the contexts in which people interact (tactical or organizational power).
4. Structural power: "By this I mean the power manifest in relationships that not only operates within settings and domains but also organizes and orchestrates the settings themselves, and that specifies the direction and distribution of energy flows."

Wolf announces his attention of focusing on structural power, which he suggests places him in the same intellectual tradition of Marx and Foucault. This itself is not without controversy, given Foucault's lack of enthusiasm for Marx's analysis of ideology (1980:58) and his declaration that he is not a Marxist (1984:385 and 1988:22).

Wolf draws on Isaiah Berlin's concept of the counter-Enlightenment in order to understand the meaning of culture that took root in anthropology. The Enlightenment promoted reason, universalism, individualism, progress—a future world, inspired by science, in which disparate cultures would give way to global uniformity, sure evidence of the psychic unity of humankind. This set in motion a counter-Enlightenment movement which glorified subjectivity, differentiation, uniqueness, tradition, and parochialism. Sympathetic to the recent critique of culture, Wolf rejects the counter-Enlightenment version, but nevertheless contends that the concept is worth saving. This is because of its "relational value" (p.67), its capacity to bring together different sectors of social life—ideas, social organization, material relations—that otherwise might be regarded as unconnected.

Wolf constructed his argument around three "extreme" or "salient" case studies—the Kwakiutl, the Aztecs, and Hitler's Germany—where ideas and power were "dramatically evident" (p.69), enhancing the prospects of understanding the connections between them. The cases are extreme in that they represent the far reaches of human variability, notably in the form of the potlatch, human sacrifice, and genocide. Kwakiutl society, dominated by what Wolf called the kin-based mode of organizing labor, was a chiefdom, stratified into aristocrats, nobles, and commoners, but did not have a centralized political structure. Status was defined by a person's genealogical proximity to the chiefly line, whose power and privilege was underwritten by the supernatural. The supernatural penetrated the material and organizational makeup of Kwakiutl society, including the ceremonial exchanges collectively known as the *potlatch*. Wolf emphasizes the enormous degree to which Kwakiutl society was transformed following contact with Europeans in the eighteenth century. Their kin-based mode of social labor succumbed to the capitalist mode, epidemics decimated the population, and a new class of competitors to the chiefs emerged, their wealth and power rooted in the marketplace. The heart of this case study concerns the reaction of the chiefs and nobles to threats to their authority, notably the manner in which they drew upon Kwakiutl ideas about the constitution of the world in order to fortify their position of privilege. In other words, ideas and power intersected for the benefit of the elite.

The Aztecs, or Tenochca, constituted the dominant city-state in central Mexico in the fifteenth century. Organized in terms of a tributary mode of social labor, Tenochca society was stratified into distinctive classes, and unlike the Kwakiutl was politically centralized. The main classes were nobles (a warrior aristocracy), merchants (plus commoners who had excelled in war), commoners (who supported the nobility with labor and the payment of tribute), and slaves. As in the case of the Kwakiutl, Wolf states that the nexus between power and ideas in Aztec culture was located in their cosmology, which penetrated and shaped virtually every aspect of material society, including the class system: "The cosmology underwrote the hierarchy of Tenochca social relations, creating a sociocosmic order wherein gods, nobles, commoners, and slaves were arranged in a graduated series with appropriate rights and obligations allocated to each distinctive grade" (pp.188–189).

Cosmological ideas also dictated warfare and human sacrifice. The Tenochca king was the nation's military ruler: "One of his first obligations following his installation was to go to war, return victoriously, and bring back prisoners to be sacrificed" (p.149). Wolf argues that human sacrifice was central to Tenochca society, and intrinsically connected to the supernatural. The gods fed humans, and humans through sacrifice fed the gods, rendering them benevolent to earthly interests, particularly those of the elite. As social change threw up new leaders, they reinterpreted cosmological ideas to show that the gods favored them. In other words, ideas were manipulated to serve class interests.

National Socialism in Germany unfolded in the era of capitalism. While Wolf acknowledges the impact of Germany's defeat in World War I, and the ensuing economic and political dislocation, his main argument is that ideas dating back to the nineteenth century laid the basis for the development of Hitler's party and its genocidal policies. As Wolf put it (p. 266): "The ideology of National Socialism that guided the Third Reich, which was largely systematized in Hitler's *Mein Kampf*, was not a 'reflection' of existing social realities. It was a medley of propositions developed during the nineteenth century, and even before, out of diverse social and economic arrangements." Paramount among these propositions were the ideas of *Volk, Race, and Fuhrer.*

Volk was an ancient idea in German history. Unlike the concept of *nation,* which was regarded as a political phenomenon, Volk was conceived as a phenomenon of nature. According to Wolf (p. 235): "*Volk* is usually translated as 'people' or 'nation,' but stands for more than that: a social entity rooted in space and time and characterized by an enduring inner essence, a spirit or *Geist,* a vital soul, which manifests itself in cultural expressions, language and art, social relations and legal codes, and even economic arrangements." As important as Volk was to Hitler's perspective, it paled next to racism. "If the Aryans were the real culture builders," Wolf writes (p. 237), "the Jews were assigned the role of paradigmatic culture destroyers." Not only did anti-Semitism stretch back to the nineteenth century, and much earlier, but so did the idea of a Fuhrer. The principle of a strongman, Wolf reveals (p. 230), who would guide the Volk to their destiny, was prominent in "the romantic pre-World War I Youth Movement." All of this reinforces his argument that the power struggles in Germany that produced National Socialism and the policy of genocide were fed by a set of ideas that dominated the German worldview in the previous century.

In the final chapter of the book, Wolf emphasizes once again that the three case studies deal with societies under stress, in each instance leading to ideologies in the service of elites. Recapitulating his basic argument, Wolf writes (p. 274): "These societies, carried forward by elites, were fashioned out of preexisting cultural materials, but they are not to be understood as disembodied cultural schemata. They addressed the very character of power in society, specifically the power that structured the differentiation, mobilization, and deployment of social labor, and they rooted that power in the nature of the cosmos."

The three case studies are presented with stunning elegance, and the author's project—the synthesis of culture and power—could hardly be more timely in view of current anthropological debates. Nevertheless, *Envisioning Power* is not an unqualified success, nor are the weak points mere sideline issues. Instead, they concern the manner in which power and culture have been conceptualized.

In this study structural power adds up to little more than a label, a concept that is brandished periodically to remind the reader that it is intended to be the focus. Rather than illuminating the data, it merely restates what is obvious in the case material: ideas interact with social relations in the context of contested patterns of advantage and disadvantage. In other words, structural power, at least in this study, is a redundant and expendable concept. The explanation, I think, is pretty obvious. Wolf selected the Kwakuitl, the Aztecs, and National Socialism because they were societies in crisis, dramatic examples of the interplay between ideas and power. My argument is that the choice of case studies was unfortunate. As indicated in the previous chapter, numerous writers have pointed out that power and conflict are intrinsically connected, almost identical twins. The implication is that it was virtually impossible *not* to find power embedded in the three cases. As societies in crisis, they were saturated in power; power dripped from them. That is why the author's periodic reminders about power strike one as gratuitous. Given the conflict-ridden nature of the three cases, what would have been novel is the demonstration that they were *not* permeated with power.

The blatant presence of power in the case studies also may account for another peculiarity of the study: the virtual absence of the array of concepts usually employed when analyzing power (authority, manipulation, force, etc.) Surprisingly, in view of Foucault's current popularity, Wolf ignores resistance, and except for brief comments (pp. 54–57 and p. 283) has little to say about discourse. He also made little use of the subtle concepts in the transactional version of political anthropology such as faction, core, middlemen, and arena, perhaps because of the transactionalists' supposed opposition to structural explanations. Yet the main reason for the conceptual parsimony may be that it took so little effort to identify power. In these conflict-drenched case studies, power stood out like a bull on a hilltop.

This is not, let it be stressed, an argument against structural power *per se*, or structural analysis in general. Consider, for example, the issue of racism. Its key dimension is its structural or systemic character. However, if one launched a study of the Ku Klux Klan, it would not add much to periodically observe that racism was implicated. That would be all too apparent.

The other problem concerns the conception of culture. In his preface Wolf observes that anthropologists have tended to view culture without power, while other social scientists have viewed ideology without culture. This makes little logical sense. If ideas are cultural phenomena, and if ideology consists of the fusion of ideas and power, then ideology by definition has one foot in culture. Certainly an analytic distinction can be made between ideas and ideology, which is precisely what Wolf (p. 4) does. By ideas he means "the entire range of mental constructs rendered manifest in public representations." By ideology he means "unified schemes or configurations developed to underwrite or manifest power." What is implied in *Envisoning Power* is that a distinction can be made between ideas linked to power which equals ideology, and ideas linked to power which is not reduced to ideology. This distinction appears to be useful partly because not all ideas linked to power develop into "a unified scheme," and also because it is consistent with current approaches to power. Indeed, if the idea-power link did not exist independent of ideology, terms such as discourse and hegemony, and the counter-discipline of culture studies, would lack purpose; ideological analysis, long entrenched in the social sciences, would already have done the job.

From the point of view of some scholars, including old-fashioned Marxists, this last sentence might be pretty close to the truth. For example, in Weber's *The Protestant Ethic and the Spirit of Capitalism* (1958), the values associated with Calvinism were said to foster capitalism; in other words, cultural phenomena penetrated the material realm and shifted the trajectory of society, implying a link between ideas and power distinct from ideology. Yet arguably more satisfactory is the explanation of Calvinism provided by Marx. Pointing out that the major ideological support for feudalism was provided by the Catholic church (see Selsam et al. 1970:255–256), he interpreted the Protestant Reformation as a necessary prelude to the emergence of capitalism.

More problematic is the causal weight that Wolf assigns to culture. He takes the position that Marx and Weber complement each other, and states that he does not assign priority to either the materialist or ideational realm. Yet if there is a consistent rendition on the role played by ideas in *Envisioning Power*, it is that they carry greater causal weight than anything else. And there is something else: more often than not, culture itself is reduced to ideas. This may have made it easier to mount an argument that power is intrinsically connected to culture without resurrecting the latter's image as an all-embracing holistic entity. But if ideas are all there is to culture, one might wonder whether the battle to salvage it is worth the trouble.

Perhaps anticipating these kinds of reactions, early in the book (p. 8) Wolf remarks that some readers may be surprised at the direction of his argument, but insists that it is consistent with his previous interests. Yet while political economy was clearly the backbone of *Europe and the People without History*, in *Envisioning Power* ideas are allowed to stand on their own as independent variables. Max Weber, despite explicitly stating that his aim in the *Protestant Ethic* was merely to demonstrate the rich congruence between the values of Calvinism and capitalism, and that he had no intention of replacing a previous one-sided argument (Marxian materialism) with another, nevertheless has often been interpreted as an idealist. To the extent that Wolf treats ideas as the key feature of human existence, his study too invites the idealist label.[6]

SOCIAL STRUCTURE AND POWER

How did social structure, the master concept in British social anthropology, manage to escape attack while culture was pounded from all directions? The quick answer is that it didn't, but before turning to the record, I suppose another question should be asked: does anybody even remember something called social structure? So overwhelming has been the discourse on culture that almost everything else in the vicinity has been driven into the shadows.

Significantly, many of the same flaws and ambiguities that have marred culture have been attributed to social structure: timelessness, boundedness, homogeneity, integration, stability, and consensus. What was missing were the usual no-shows: conflict, change, and power. Just as there was no single definition of culture even in the era of Boas and Sapir, the same has been true for social structure. Social anthropologists from the time of Radcliffe-Brown have debated whether social structure was an empirical or analytic concept (that is, a concrete entity or merely a logical construct or heuristic device); whether society was a bounded system within a specific geographical space, or a borderless fiction; whether history, the individual and social change could be accommodated, or were romantic diversions incompatible with scientific inquiry.

Following World War II, Gluckman (1956) appeared to turn the tables on structural functionalism by shifting the focus from harmony and consensus to conflict and dissensus. Yet by arguing that strains in society tended to cancel each other out, and that conflict was actually functional since it contributed to overall solidarity, his approach ended up as just another version of the equilibrium model, leaving social structure largely unscathed. The transactional barrage against structural functionalism was much more successful. Emphasizing conflict, change, power struggle, multiple and contradictory norms, and the impact of the innovative and manipulative individual, the transactionalists reduced social structure to an ideological smokescreen which concealed how human beings actually interacted.[7] With social structure down and wounded, postmodernism and feminist anthropology put it out of its misery. Structure and behavior gave way to meaning and interpretation, particularism and the life history displaced generalization and model, and power hitchhiked a ride with discourse into the heart of the anthropological universe.

There is no reason, however, to celebrate the demolition of social structure, at least if socio-cultural anthropology wants to claim its own conceptual territory. If culture can potentially be resuscitated by power, perhaps the same holds true for social structure. When power enters culture we get ideology. When power penetrates social structure we get stratification. But it is precisely here that caution is advised. This is because a focus on power and stratification does not inevitably highlight inequality. Parsons, it will be recalled, referred to power as a resource in the service of the collective good. He also (1964:329) has portrayed stratification as society's backbone, its source of integration and stability.

It would also be a mistake to assume that stratification has a greater, or more natural, affinity to social structure than to culture. The main divisions within social structure in social anthropology have been kinship, economy, polity, and religion—not class, gender, and race. Moreover, until the 1960s or so, the overwhelming emphasis was on egalitarianism: hunters and gatherers without the burden of an economic surplus, peasants competing to remain equal, peace in the feud, balanced segmentary opposition. M.G. Smith (1966:154) has claimed that in contrast to sociologists like Parsons, anthropologists have not assumed that stratification has been universal. Smith does not deny that inequality exists on the basis of age, sex, and kinship, or that positions of differential status aren't present in all societies. But in his mind these do not add up to stratification because they merely reflect family organization; besides, in non-stratified societies almost everyone eventually becomes eligible for high status positions.

Whatever the merits of Smith's arguments, we are now in the era of the nation-state and globalization, and there can be no question about the relevancy of stratification and its principal components. In the pages that follow I shall focus on racism. In doing so I do not wish to imply that class and gender are unrelated to racism or somehow less important. Racism arguably is simply an ideological mechanism which props up the ruling class by dividing the proletariat; and as Montagu pointed out long ago (1957:39), sexual prejudice is remarkably similar to racial prejudice.[8] There exists, however, an enormous literature on gender, both within and beyond anthropology; and while it was only a decade ago that Ortner (1991:166) complained that Western anthropologists working at home were blind to class, we may have turned the corner, thanks in part to the focus on globalization. The big hole remains the investigation of racism. Whether anthropologists think that racism lies beyond the boundaries of their discipline, is a thing of the past, or simply too hot to handle, one thing is certain: the amount of attention paid to racism has been minuscule, and appears to be diminishing by the decade.

THE OSTRICH SYNDROME

There was a time, long ago, when leading figures in anthropology (Boas and Benedict) and in sociology (Ward, Ross, and Park) put the analysis of racism at the top of the agenda. While Montagu, Harris, Little, Banton, and Rex continued the tradition, for most anthropologists today racism appears to be about as relevant as the number of rocks on the moon. Reflecting on the degree to which the topic of racism is currently avoided, Shanklin (1998) and Mukhopadhyay and Moses (1997) observe that in both physical and cultural anthropology there appears to be a "no race" policy, or at least a "no discussion" of race. The consequence, Shanklin points out, is that anthropology students have been left with the impression that the discipline has nothing to say about the phenomenon.[9]

Could it be that the race concept (and racism) has finally faded away, the pleasant outcome of the victory of culture over biology? Improbable—even within the university setting. In a survey conducted in the mid-1980s (Lieberman et al. 1992), 75 percent of biologists and 50 percent of physical anthropologists agreed that biological races exist within the species Homo sapiens; in an earlier study, almost one-third of cultural anthropologists did likewise.[10] Lieberman and his collaborators were impressed by the fact that the evidence showed a gradual decrease in the belief of separate human races since the 1930s, as measured by textbook context. What I find startling is that such a large percentage of physical and cultural anthropologists continue to embrace the notion.

Ironically, Boas may be at the heart of the problem. By separating race and culture, and treating race as a neutral biological concept, he helped, according to Visweswaran (1998), to legitimate the scientific study of race, opening the way to scientific racism. Montagu, a student of Boas, argued that the concept of race itself was racist. In this context Visweswaran has suggested that what Boas failed to appreciate was that the meaning of biological concepts such as race is conditioned by the social and political environment.

Montagu's solution was to replace race by ethnic group, but this too is problematic. Not only does it de-politicize race relations, but it also obscures the fact that not all ethnic groups are equal: skin color and national origin do make a difference when it comes to realizing the American Dream. The issue of ethnicity transports us into the realm of culture. A number of writers, Wolf included (1994), have argued that ethnic studies materialized in the 1960s because culture was incapable of coping with internal division. Others (Visweswaran, for example) have claimed that racism became the subject matter of multicultural and cultural studies because cultural anthropology had nothing to say about it. Even more damning, several critics, as pointed out in Chapter One, have argued that culture (and ethnic group) has become a substitute term for race. If this is so, race-thinking is very widespread indeed, judged by the current popularity of the culture construct both within and beyond the academy.[11]

Let us give the final word to the master, Claude Lévi-Strauss (1994:423–424): "You know of my attraction for Japan. Whenever I'm in the metro in Paris and I see a couple that looks Japanese, I look at them with interest and sympathy, ready to give them a hand. Is that racism?" Well, maybe not, but there certainly is a whiff of it in the air. Lévi-Strauss then adds that everyone thinks as he does, and states: "I belong to a culture that has a distinctive lifestyle and value system, so cultures that are extremely different don't automatically appeal to me." What a remarkable confession of ethnocentrism. Visweswaran has suggested that anthropologists have failed to take a leadership role in recent years in the fight against racism because they believe that they have led the battle all along, reflected in their commitment to relativism and culture. The example of Lévi-Strauss, however, suggests that there may be a less positive motive for the "no race discussion" policy, or what I prefer to label "the ostrich syndrome."[12]

CONCEPTUALIZING RACISM

Omi and Winant (1986) have reduced the various approaches to racism to three major paradigms: ethnicity, class, and nation. When ethnicity, by far the dominant paradigm, emerged in the 1920s it contained a progressive tinge by virtue of its opposition to the prevailing biological conception of race. In the 1970s and 1980s it was taken over by the neoconservative camp, bent on opposing the more radical class and nation paradigms, and especially the argument that group rights outweigh individual ones.[13] A major flaw in all three paradigms, the authors argue, is that they are reductionist. Rather than being autonomous, racism is watered down to ethnic group, with the emphasis on eventual assimilation, or to class informed by economic relations and nation shaped by colonialism. The ambitious aim of Omi and Winant is to erect a paradigm in which racism is a force in its own right. To this they give the label "racial formation." American society, in their judgment, is permeated by racism. Racism informs every identity, social practice, and institution. It is coterminous with the state, and rather than being epiphenomenal to class (or anything else), it shapes class relations.

No doubt Omi and Winant are correct that reductionism has plagued the three main paradigms, but their solution is not beyond criticism. I have no quarrel with the ideas behind racial formation—the sheer extent and range of racism in American society. But where does this racism come from? What perpetuates it? One wonders if we can even begin to answer these questions without retreating to some sort of reductionism. There is another small problem, quite an ironic one. Members of the Ku Klux Klan and the Aryan Nations would be delighted with the work of Omi and Winant. It confirms what they have contended all along—that racism is the single most dominant force in society, that the history of the world is the history of race relations.[14]

Assuming that there is little to lose (except perhaps my reputation), I have tried my own hand at conceptualizing racism, dividing the scheme into three levels:

1. Basic Preconditions (panhuman predispositions)
   - ethnocentrism
   - scapegoating
   - xenophobia
   - sexual competition
   - species insecurity
   - inherent mental classificatory propensity
2. General Social Structural-Power Determinants (historically specific phenomena)
   - colonialism
   - capitalism
   - nationalism
   - mass communications (media portrayal)
3. Specific Triggering Mechanisms (immediate social events)
   - downward swings in the economy
   - changes in immigration patterns
   - celebrated incidents of minority persecution or privilege
   - momentous national and international political strains

The basic preconditions are not confined to time and space; they are among the criteria that define Homo sapiens. They do not inevitably lead to racism; instead they provide a background environment out of which society could develop in numerous directions, including a racist one. The general social determinants, all of them historically rooted and linked to power, make it somewhat more possible that the direction taken will be racist. The specific triggering mechanisms are examples of what can set racism in motion, given numbers one and two above.

In terms of sheer logic the causal direction implied in the scheme, from level one through two and three, makes sense, because obviously the components in the first level predate those in the other levels. In theoretical terms, however, the scheme is misleading. This is because all of the elements described as basic preconditions are shaped by the social and political forces in level two. This is especially obvious in relation to ethnocentrism, scapegoating, and xenophobia, but no less true for the other elements. Stember (1976) and Jahoda (1961) have pointed to sexual competition as one of the major sources of racism; the calculation of preferred and unpreferred mates is unavoidably based on the forces of history and differential power. Species insecurity, the flip side of human sensitivity, partly explains the vulnerability for simplicity, such as racial classification; who gets slotted at the top and the bottom, however, is once again a matter of historical social and political forces. Inherent mental classificatory propensity is somewhat more ambiguous. Durkheim and Mauss (1963) contended that no such propensity exists. Their argument was that only when people became organized into groups did they begin to classify things, and the emerging taxonomies reflected the properties of their social structures. Even if we agree with Needham (1979) that classification is indeed an intrinsic mental faculty, that says nothing about its empirical content. In other words, whether classifications take a racist twist or not is determined by the social and political environment. My argument, then, is that the key to the scheme is level two. The dominant causal lines flow from this level to the others. In arguing such, I have merely aligned myself with Visweswaran, who criticized Boas for failing to realize that the meaning of the concept of race was socially and politically conditioned, not the neutral scientific term that he envisaged.

It has been asserted (Baker 1978:316, Benedict 1960:148, Hughes and Kallen 1974:105) that racism is essentially a power contest. In the above conceptual scheme, power does not exhaust the explanation of racism, but it is the fundamental factor. This scheme may help to clarify a couple of the most contentious issues in the literature. One concerns the status of racism as an independent entity. The conventional Marxist perspective (Cox 1948) is that racism is an epiphenomenon of class, a mechanism that divides the workers along color lines for the benefit of the owners. The conventional liberal perspective (Rex 1970) accepts all this, but insists that racism is to some degree a thing in itself; in other words it contains an autonomous zone irreducible to the class system. The other contentious issue is the assertion that only white people can be and are racists. The reasoning is that above all else racism is an expression of power, which white people monopolize.

While Marxists are inclined to dismiss the liberal version of racism as so much nonsense, something impossible to articulate, what might be meant by the autonomous zone are the several pan-human psychological propensities. These same propensities might help to remove some of the controversy regarding the claim that only white people can be racists. Racism does revolve primarily around power, but complementing power are elements like ethnocentrism, scapegoating, and xenophobia, and they can invade the minds of human beings everywhere.

This conceptual scheme, aimed at the macro level of society, obviously is less sensitive at the institutional and micro levels of interaction. Several years ago I embarked on an investigation of multiculturalism as it related to the institution of sports. I had just completed a study of organized racism and anti-Semitism, which had left me depressed. For my next project I wanted something positive. What I latched onto was the idea of examining the participation of Third World youth in the game of ice hockey, which I thought would celebrate their presence in Canada. Two assumptions guided the conception of the study. One was that a large number of young people from Third World countries had picked up the game. This assumption was based on personal knowledge; some of the children of friends who had emigrated to Canada from Africa and the West Indies were dashing across the ice surface, sticks in hand. The other assumption was that sports are based more on merit than possibly any other institution; or, put negatively, less affected by ascriptive criteria such as class and race. After all, statistics on performance are printed in the daily newspapers.

Brimming with confidence that the unfolding story would portray race relations in a positive light, I turned to the literature and ran head-on into a major controversy: whether or not athletic capacity varies with race. Of course, if the concept of race was meaningless, as anthropologists have argued, so too was the controversy. Nevertheless, in an article in *Sports Illustrated* (Kane 1971) entitled "An Assessment of 'Black Is Best'," it was contended that African-origin people have a genetic advantage in athletic endeavors. Harry Edwards, a leading figure in the sociology of sport, countered Kane's argument by stating (1974) that the large number of African Americans in sports such as football and basketball was proof once and for all that racism pervades American society. They are driven towards sports for a simple reason: other institutions are closed to them. It could be argued, as it often is, that this is not all bad: success is sports is the one sure avenue to upward class mobility. Yet following the Los Angeles riots in 1992, James Brown, former football star turned actor, condemned the emphasis on sports among African Americans as one of the principal causes of underachievement. Rather than becoming doctors, plumbers, and storekeepers— the mundane occupations of other ethnic groups—they aspired to careers as professional athletes, which only a handful would ever realize.

Although Edwards' critique was highly plausible, in the late 1990s another article appeared in *Sports Illustrated* (unattributed 1997) entitled "What Ever Happened to the White Athlete?" The message once again was that genetically based racial differences explained black athletic superiority, but there was a greater recognition that scientific evidence for this interpretation was scanty (see also Hoberman 1997).

In addition to the controversial argument about race-linked athletic advantage, the literature consistently contradicted the assumption that sports are immune to racism. This was not a promising beginning for my study, nor did the situation improve when I began attending games and interviewing players, coaches, parents, and fans. Within a few months of sporadic field work (I was teaching at the time) I realized that Third World youth had not flocked to the game of ice hockey; in fact, the majority of those who were involved were at least third-generation Canadians. Much to my chagrin, I was also forced to accept that hockey was much less impervious to racism than anticipated. To give only a single example, in one game between teenagers, a black player was taunted to such a degree that the coaches withdrew their teams from the ice. Even in professional hockey, stories abounded (Wallace 1988) about the harsh treatment of the first black players to make the grade, and about others with abundant talent who had been buried in the minor leagues.

That the institution of sports harbors racism should come as no surprise, because it is as much a part of society as the school and the workplace (Gruneau 1982), and presumably equally susceptible to the elements outlined in my conceptual scheme.[15] This was not, however, the positive study that I had wanted, and within a few months I discarded it, but not before discovering another intriguing phenomenon: the existence in the Toronto area of several ethnic-based hockey teams and even hockey leagues. Usually two "imports" per team were allowed, defined as anyone not sharing a team's ethnic origins. Was this multiculturalism at its best, or multiculturalism gone wild? Were people drawn to these teams because of ethnic identity, or because the climate was inhospitable in the mainstream leagues? On what basis could it be argued that ethnicity was a legitimate criterion for team or league membership? In grappling with this last question, I turned to Steward's core-periphery distinction. It seemed that when sports constituted "work," as in professional hockey, they belong to the core, where achievement and universalistic criteria operated, rendering ethnic preference illegitimate; but when sports constituted "play," as in amateur hockey, they fell into the periphery where ascriptive and particularistic criteria were allowed.

Power, too, was relevant, because all the ethnic teams consisted of minority groups; presumably, had a dominant ethnic group such as English-Canadians attempted to form its own league, there would have been an uproar. This does not mean, however, that association on the basis of ethnicity in the realm of leisure and play only occurs among minority groups. To the contrary, if we want to get a clear reading of the quality of race and ethnic relations in a society and the degree of assimilation, we would do well to look closely at what happens when the factory shuts down for the day and the office lights are turned off. Leisure space, in other words, is where ethnic bonds in general prevail, and it may well be the last refuge of the racist.

When we drop from the institutional to the individual level, analysis becomes even more complicated. Panhuman constraints such as ethnocentrism and xenophobia obviously still operate, as do social and political forces, and the arrival of a boatload of illegal immigrants can quickly bring latent racism out into the open. However, an additional variable has to be entertained: the individual personality. For example, in a town in rural Ontario (Barrett 1994), a teacher in the secondary school was consistently identified by minority students as a racist. When I interviewed him, he candidly stated that some of the African-Canadian and Aboriginal students were difficult to handle, but argued it had nothing to do with race; instead it was a question of poverty and home life, especially in single-parent families. He also described his style as authoritarian, and declared that he runs his classroom like an army camp. The possibility exists, I suppose, that what some of his students interpreted as racism was nothing more than his forceful personality.

It sometimes is thought that if only people of different ethnic backgrounds could get to know each other, racism would disintegrate, because its basis is ignorance. This bring us to another individual in the rural Ontario town—a middle-aged woman whose best friend was a younger African-Canadian woman. This latter person, who owned a store, had run into her share of obstacles with the town council. Her older friend was enraged, interpreting the situation as one of racism. Yet I discovered a peculiar side to this older woman. Despite her friendship with the other woman, she was far from free of the racist bug. On a rare visit to Toronto she spotted people of color everywhere. She couldn't believe what had happened to the city, and remarked that she feared for her safety. The implication is clear: this woman certainly was bosom pals with a person of color, but when she generalized to the world at large it was not that relationship but instead (dare I suggest it) the various elements in my abstract conceptual scheme that shaped her judgment.

CONCLUSION

As a frame of reference or general descriptive term there is nothing especially objectionable about culture, and the same holds for social structure, which Kroeber, if my memory serves me well, once referred to as a source of pleasant puzzlement. However, both culture and social structure are tools intended for the lazy academic. Just as Worsley (1970) argued that charisma is a substitute for explanation, and must be decoded to expose the underlying values, interests, and social and political forces, the same can be said about culture and social structure. If this is not done, both concepts constitute analytic quick fixes, with the probable consequence of reinforcing the ideological mainstream.

The risk, of course, is that by digging beneath these surface concepts, they might be undermined. That would be unfortunate. There is every reason to retain culture and social structure, and thus continuity with the discipline's past, if one condition is met: the welcome mat is put out for power. With power embraced, neither ideology nor stratification can be overlooked. It follows that in attempting to fuse culture and power, Wolf was right on the money. If his efforts are not beyond criticism, that is hardly surprising. Some of the best minds in the previous generation (see Lenski 1966, and several of the articles in Demerath and Peterson 1967) tried to synthesize the consensus and conflict models, but came up short. The fusion of culture and power is much the same project.

NOTES

1. That may well be correct, but as Harris has pointed out (1979), every time a macaque or chimpanzee is observed in a cultural performance, it is worth a journal article, but all the journals and libraries in the world could not keep track of ongoing human cultural performances.

2. Edgerton was especially critical of Geertz's contribution to the position of epistemological relativism in which cultures are incommensurate, each in a world of its own. It is thus fitting that Geertz took up the challenge posed by the anti-relativists. Although his critique (1984) is beautifully written, even by his standards, I doubt whether it would persuade anyone to switch camps. This is because it doesn't do much more than to articulate the competing viewpoints.

3. Yet in his later study of nationalism, Hobsbawm (1990:9–12), like Gellner (1983:56), appears to regard the falsified and fictionalized cultural past often fashioned by nationalists as somewhat pejorative.

4. For an excellent sample of the wide range of viewpoints on culture in early anthropology, see Freilich (1972).

5. Geertz, incidentally, also (1973:49) mounted a remarkably succinct and learned defense of Culture, arguing that without the capacity for symbolic thinking human beings "would be unworkable monstrosities."

6. For a more elaborate version of this critique of *Envisioning Power*, see Barrett, Stokholm, and Burke (2001).

7. While there is considerable overlap between social structure and structural functionalism, they are not identical, the one being a concept, the other a theoretical perspective. This explains how it can be that the transactionalists' attack on structural functionalism was also an attack on social structure, while Gluckman's attempt to demolish structural functionalism left social structure intact. Similarly, in the Marxian conflict model, contradiction, mode of production, technology, and economy claim most of the conceptual space, but room still is made for social structure.

8. In a revealing article, Lieberman (1997) has shown that women in anthropology took the lead over men in deconstructing the race concept.

9. Shanklin reveals that Foucault had planned to write a book called *Population and Races*. Although the project was never completed, tapes of his lectures at the Collège de France indicate that he considered race to be sexuality's twin, both of them instruments of bio-power at the disposal of state discourse.

10. Reported in Mukhopadhyay and Moses (1997:522).

11. Willis (1972) has put the case against anthropology much more bluntly. Not only, in his judgment, was the evolutionary perspective of Morgan and Tylor implicitly racist,

but he also suggests that Boas's real target may have been anti-Semitism rather than racism, and that ethnographers had so little to say about field work in the past because it was essentially a racist experience.

12. When I was conducting research on organized racism in Canada (Barrett 1987), I interviewed the principal of a secondary school who decided not to confront a teacher who espoused racist and anti-Semitic views in the classroom because they didn't affect him personally; besides, to do so, in the principal's judgment, would only have exacerbated the problem. That was the ostrich syndrome in action.

13. For an earlier overview of these paradigms, especially the colonial one, see Prager's important article (1972).

14. Of course, unlike Omi and Winant they think that is marvellous.

15. Hargreaves (1982:121) has referred to sports in contemporary society as the new opiate of the people. My female graduate students agree that that may be true for men, but not for women.

Chapter 4

The Explanatory Limits of Power

The less power is focused on in sociocultural analysis, the more probable that dominant discourses will be accepted at face value, that ideology will be confused with objective knowledge, that the status quo will be regarded as natural and just, and that consensus will overshadow conflict. Power, therefore, is important. Yet power, like culture and social structure, bears its share of ambiguity and contradiction, with little agreement among scholars about what it means or explains. If the focus on power is going to be anything more than a short-lived fad, we must recognize its limitations and attempt to overcome them, rather than blowing up the concept only to watch it deflate. Toward this end, 20 assumptions about power are introduced, most of them familiar to both social scientists and lay people. As it will be shown, for every assumption about power, there is a plausible counter-assumption. The implication is that power is no less complex and slippery than other key concepts in the social sciences.

BASIC ASSUMPTIONS

1. Power is the most fundamental human motive. Karl Marx and conventional economists, according to Bertrand Russell, have assumed that the basic human motive is self-interest, but have been wrong. Power warrants that distinction. In Russell's words (1938:13, 15, 263), power is "the fundamental concept " and "chief motive" dealt with in the social sciences, and "an essential part of human nature." Edmund Leach (1954:10), no doubt with the cross-cultural perspective in mind, remarked that we are never justified in assuming that behavior can be reduced to a single motive—except, that is, for power.

As a psychological phenomenon, power could be a pan-human drive, but still vary in degree from one individual to the next. Russell (1938:14) observed that some people are "exceptionally power-loving," which Laswell (see Emmet 1971:85) attempted to explain as a form of pathology. Such people, he contended, suffered as children, and chase after power and political position to compensate for infantile deprivations.

But: While recognizing that the idea of a power drive, a will to power, or a lust for power has deep roots in Western thought, Wrong, like Hobbes, argued that power is only a means to other ends such as wealth and prestige, and concluded (1979:236): "the concept of a quasi-biological or universally human psychological drive is neither tenable nor a useful one." As for the pathological nature of power-seekers, Dahl says it is contradicted by the fact that people who strive for power do not fall into a distinctive personality type. Russell seems to cast doubt on his own argument by stating that the impulse of submission is just as prevalent as the drive for power, although I suppose it could be countered that they are the opposite sides of a single dialectic.

2. Power is virtually coterminous with society. Power is not a psychological motive at all. It is a sociological phenomenon, unrestrained and ubiquitous, implicated in all institutions, roles, beliefs, values, and norms; it runs through class, gender, and ethnicity, but is deeper and broader than any one of them. This, in essence, is a portrait of structural power, that which is embedded in society, conforms to the shape of the stratification system, and is unmotivated or unintentional. The sheer weight of the social structure reproduces the pattern of advantage and disadvantage over time independent of human volition. It is because power permeates the entire sociocultural fabric that social scientists have had so much difficulty coping with it theoretically. To explain power is tantamount to explaining society.

But: The above argument contains a serious logical flaw. If power is equivalent to society, if it is everything, then it lacks explanatory value. This is because it is a constant across the field of human interaction, and a constant cannot explain variation. As McClelland (1971:44) observed: "Not everything can be power; we must have at least one other class, perhaps to be called *not-power*, to provide some contrast for comparison."

There are other problems such as the assumption that the consequences of power struggles are predetermined by the nature of the stratification system. As Bendix pointed out long ago (1953), there is too much indeterminacy in human interaction to support that assumption; in other words, people do not necessarily behave politically as their class position would suggest. Structural power implies formal role structure and formal rules of behavior. This, too, has drawn criticism, especially from the transactionalists who portray the formal system as a smokescreen for the semi-chaos of actual behavior. Then there are the writers, probably the majority, who prefer a voluntaristic conception of power over a structural one. Wrong (1979) restricts power to intentional and effective acts not only because he thinks that is what power is all about, but also because if power was extended to unintentional acts—that is, to structural power—it would be equivalent to the entire sociological territory, and thus useless.

3. *Power in its most elementary form is force.* Might is right. Revolutions are the locomotives of history. Power comes out of the barrel of a gun. The state has a monopoly over the instruments of force. Armed combat in the service of national liberation is necessary not only because there is no other way but also in order to eradicate the ideological muck of colonial mentality. Although C. Wright Mills (1967:23) points to authority, manipulation, and coercion as the three main types of power, he states that "coercion is the 'final' form of power."

But: What about the power of the pen, the assertion that knowledge is power? Or Gramsci's and Lenin's (Selsam et al. 1970:363–364) twin elements of force and consent, with the qualification (also made by Russell) that force must be used sparingly, otherwise it might backfire. Or the position taken by prominent authors (who possess "authority"!) such as Parsons, Arendt, and Foucault that force has nothing to do with power—where force is found power is not.

Bailey (1980:6) has suggested that persuasion is more basic than force. Persuasion includes "the whole conventional range from outright and overt force at one corner to rational argument at another, and, at the third, some devious maneuver or manipulation." Russell doesn't mount the same argument, but he does question the distinction between force and other types of power, stating (1938:268), "Many forms of persuasion ... are really a kind of force." Then there is the observation made by Swartz, Turner, and Tuden (1976:9): "Despite its undeniable importance, insuperable difficulties confront the view that force is the sole, or even the major, basis of political behavior."

4. *Power is always negative, destructive, unfair, immoral.* Power is the key component of the stratification system. It connotes one person or one sector of society lording it over another. It produces and sustains institutionalized inequality, such as men over women in a patriarchal society, or white people over people of color during South Africa's apartheid era and, less dramatically, in nations such as the United States and Canada. Patterns of advantage and disadvantage are propped up by ideology, with negative sanctions, especially force, never far in the background.

Here we find the assumption that power is an unfair resource, as, for example, when a person "pulls rank" in order to get her or his way. Another assumption is that power-hungry people are morally flawed. Often, indeed, ambitious individuals must pretend (at least during the early stages of the game) that they don't want power, whether it is the presidency of a country or the chair of a university department. If they don't play by these rules, the audience may begin to wonder whether their values are distorted. Of course, they can claim that the groundswell of support for their candidacy was too overwhelming to ignore; and when they do get into office they can finesse the discourse so that what constitutes negative power is the irresponsible clique in the university department that challenged them, or the radicals in the defeated opposition party, with their half-baked socialist or right-wing agenda (it doesn't matter which—either slur will stick).

But: Could an orchestra produce soul-tingling music without the power and authority of the conductor to lead it? How effective would a football team be without a quarterback (even if the plays are piped in by the coach)? The implication is that differential power and authority are not by definition destructive. Parsons, of course, put the case in favor of power much more strongly: power is always legitimate in that it is exercised for the common good. Nor has he been the only prominent scholar to argue along these lines. Etzioni (1993:23) wrote: "we view societal power as a form of the mobilization of societal energy in the service of societal goals." Russell suggests that power is only negative if it is desired as an end in itself; if sought after as a means to bring benefit to others, it is pure and positive. Remarking that the appropriate response to the public statements of aspiring political leaders is often deep cynicism, Galbraith nevertheless adds that power is "socially essential." The reason that power has got such a bad rap, contends Dahl, is that the literature has been deeply biased; it has focused mostly on negative sanctions and conflict, ignoring positive sanctions, consensus, and collective benefits.

5. *Raw or naked power is illegitimate; authority is legitimate.* This, of course, corresponds to Weber's distinction between power and authority. If authority, or institutionalized power, did not exist, would society possess sufficient cohesion and stability to persist?

But: Effective power doesn't have to be legitimate power, nor is consensus the only basis of leadership—witness the prevalence of military regimes. Moreover, institutionalized power or authority is essentially ideology which serves the interests of the class or party capable of defining what is legitimate. In other words, authority looks very much like manipulation, because it depends on members of the other classes unwittingly acquiescing to interests that are not their own. As for power being illegitimate, we have already seen that Parsons and others would strongly disagree.

Moreover, something quite intriguing transpires when raw and naked power are decoded. They seem to carry the connotations of elementary power, undisguised by human custom; in other words, pre-cultural or natural power. Their literal opposites are cooked or clothed power. Cooked power, like "cooked" data, suggests phony, manipulated power, and clothed power implies power dressed up to deceive. In other words, raw or naked power takes on the connotations of open, honest, true power, while cooked or clothed power resembles ideologically conditioned authority. This comes very close to implying that guileless non-institutionalized power is legitimate, while deceptive institutionalized power is not.

6. *Power always conceals itself.* The idea here is that power is slippery, sneaky, exercised without people's awareness. Concealed power is closely associated with propaganda, ideology, and manipulation. Galbraith stated (1983:12): "much exercise of power depends on a social conditioning that seeks to conceal it." He

added that concealed power is more prevalent in contemporary society than at any other period in history. Harris wrote (1971:420): "The nature of contemporary class structures is the object of elaborate ideological manipulation by the ruling classes of modern industrial states. Both the United States and the Soviet Union, for example, have ruling classes that employ every conceivable artifice to foster the illusion that they do not exist." Russell comments on one type of concealed power: that exercised by individuals in the back rooms of political parties. Such people, he charges, are tainted, more in love with power than glory.

But: Foucault has written (1978:86) that "power is tolerable only on condition that it mask a substantial part of itself." Moreover, he adds, this is beneficial for both the dominator and the dominated, presumably because power is required in order for society to function.

Power also is exercised merely by revealing itself, such as a show of armaments in a military parade (the threat rather than the application of power). Some individuals, indeed, like to display their power. For example, on a pleasant spring morning, with the mist still rising off the lake, my father pulled in a lunker. Almost immediately another fishing boat approached us, and without any show of identification, and no visible signs of authority such as a game-warden's garb, the man at the motor curtly ordered that the fish be thrown back into the lake (the season for that species was still a couple of weeks away). Although we complied, and obviously would have allowed the fish its liberty without being compelled to do so—obviously, I repeat—the arrogance of power detracted briefly from the day's pleasure.

7. *Power corrupts.* The reasons, I think, that the electorate in Western democracies votes a ruling party out of office have less to do with ideology than with the fact that citizens simply grow jaded with the old faces and want to see fresh ones; and, more importantly, because once a party has been in office for a couple of terms it begins to act as if it were royalty, above the rules and ethics that apply to ordinary mortals. Arrogance, conceit, and deviousness are the psychological components of enduring political supremacy.

But: Without power where would the women's movement, the anti-racist movement, gay and lesbian rights, and the advancement of people with disabilities be today? Conversely, lacking power, think of the increasing misery of poor people and poor nations in the age of globalization. Even at the level of the individual, power at times can be salutary. A hockey player with unfulfilled promise sometimes will raise his game to star level after the captain's "C" is pinned on his jersey (of course, the opposite can also occur). And surely we all can think of the woman or man who sheds the shackles of self-doubt, and indeed blossoms, after assuming the trappings of higher office, usually as a result of the encouragement of others.

8. *Knowledge is power.* To paraphrase Marx, the ideas of the ruling class are the ruling ideas; the class that is the dominant material force is also the dominant intellectual force. For Said in *Orientalism* (1979), there is no knowledge divorced from power. For Gramsci (see Merrington 1968), intellectuals are

experts in legitimation; they render the ruling class's dominance acceptable to the rest of society.

But: Remember that Foucault denied that he had ever equated knowledge and power, remarking that if they were one and the same thing he could have saved himself a lot of hard work. Anti-relativists would argue that there is objective knowledge, independent of ideological constraints. And even if knowledge does mean power, it is not necessarily for the benefit of the elite. Said's *Orientalism* itself is an example of resistance, of academic expertise being directed against privilege rather than legitimating it.

9. Knowledge of power disarms power. This has a couple of connotations. One is that if we understand how manipulation works, and can detect when it is being exercised, or when higher class interests are disguised by ideology, we should be in a better position to resist. Social scientists, given their subject matter and training, should enjoy an advantage in terms of understanding and nullifying power. The other connotation is that people who understand how power works should be immune to its seductive allure. Wisdom should elevate them above the struggles and ambitions that move mere mortals around the chessboard. Indeed, for the trained social scientist, power should even be repulsive.

But: The above comments assume that power is negative, a perspective not shared by all writers. More significantly, when it comes to their orientation to power, social scientists are "mere mortals" too, no more capable of avoiding either the impact or seductive attraction of power than anyone else. One of my great surprises, and disappointments, as a graduate student was the discovery that the vast knowledge possessed by my teachers (well, by at least some of them) appeared to make little difference in their personal lives. Many of them seemed to be as hungry for positions of high status and influence as the rest of the population, as envious of the success of their colleagues, and occasionally as viciously irrational. For example, after a close friend successfully defended his Ph.D. thesis, his supervisor, who had a reputation for giving students a hard time, commented without any apparent embarrassment that it was now my friend's turn to apply the screws to students.

At an anthropological conference a few years ago I sat in the spring sunshine on a patio with a couple of dozen colleagues. All of a sudden heads swung as if drawn by a magnet. The object of interest was a handful of the top guns in Canadian anthropology, strolling together across the campus. Accomplished scholars all of them, they no doubt warranted our attention, even if, as was likely, that had been the furthest thing from their minds. Besides, it could be argued that if women and men of great talent did not assume leadership roles, the ship would be rudderless, or fall under the control of idiots. Yet the fact remains that all that power concentrated in such a small space was hypnotic, and presumably the top guns became conscious that they were on display, and perhaps even were mildly pleased by our reaction. Then there is the alleged contradiction between knowledge and action, the notion that understanding not only can lead to wisdom but also to paralysis. A case even could be made for the infighting and irrationality that sometimes characterizes academic interaction. A life devoid of these characteristics is a life on the margins, one not experienced to the full. All of this may well be true, but it does lead us to an interesting conclusion: if we want to get a handle on the stratification system and the complexities and politics of human struggle, we do not have to step out of the academy, including the small sector inhabited by social scientists.

10. *Power is always potentially asymmetrical.* In his earlier work Parsons described power as hierarchical. Unlike money and goods in economics, it was not a matter of more or less, but rather higher and lower. Power, for Parsons, meant power *over* another.

But: While common sense suggests that power means somebody is in control and someone else is being controlled, the anthropological record indicates otherwise. In egalitarian, stateless societies based on subsistence, power is exercised and political decisions are made without institutionalizing hierarchy. Some individuals, such as the "big men" of Melanesian fame, may rise above the rest on the basis of drive, merit, and manipulation, but their power dies with them; it is not formalized in role and office. That, it may be recalled, was essentially M.G. Smith's argument regarding non-stratified, egalitarian societies.

In the transactional literature, power sometimes resembles a game in which the competitors are equally talented with similar resources, and the least important thing is the outcome. Instead the focus is on the tactics and strategies, especially those that stretch the rules and ultimately produce a victor. It is in this context, of course, that the transactional school has been criticized for losing sight of the big picture: the broader stratification system within which factional contests unfold.

11. *As democracy increases, power decreases.* This argument only makes sense if it means elite power declines, while the power of the masses increases. Power can be defined as the capacity to make choices; the greater the degree of democracy, the greater the number of people with that capacity, reflected, for example, in universal suffrage.

But: Caution must be exercised before concluding that "the people" are free and empowered. Only one type of elite power has faded: unchecked, arbitrary, tyrannical, dictatorial power, with a monopoly over and a willingness to use force. Writing in the 1930s, Bertrand Russell concluded that the state in industrial societies has much more control than it had in pre-industrial societies, and Galbraith suggests that never before in history have people been so controlled and manipulated by government-generated ideology and propaganda (what he labels conditional power) as in the modern industrial state. That too, of course, was C. Wright Mills' message: a power elite, unparalled in history, has taken over American society.

The implication is that elite power has not decreased—it merely has changed its complexion. Mann captures this change neatly with his terms *despotic* and *infrastructural* power. By despotic power he means tyrannical power; by infrastructural power he means the capacity of the state to penetrate and influence every corner of civil society. Capitalist democracies, he argues, are despotically weak but infrastructurally strong. In Mann's words (1993:315): "When people in the West today complain of the growing power of the state, they cannot be referring sensibly to the despotic powers of the state elite itself, for if anything these are still declining. . . . But the complaint is more justly levelled against the state's encroachments. These powers are now immense. . . . The state penetrates everyday life more than did any historical state."

Few academic ideas survive very long, as social change rolls on, and that applies to Mann's argument. With the emergence of globalization and multinational corporations, not only has the power of the masses been further eroded, reflected in the growing gap between rich and poor, but so too has the power of the state.

12. *Power equals discourse.* Discourse straddles knowledge and power; it bridges the text and the concrete world; it focuses our attention on how a text is framed in order to covertly promote vested interests. Sometimes discourse analysis is made easier by the presence of key words or expressions. For example, while in my judgment there are several compelling reasons for rallying behind the state of Israel, the foremost being the Holocaust, American government spokespeople almost always refer to Israel as a "democracy," as if that, rather than the long history of anti-Semitism, justifies their support. Yet during the Cold War it didn't seem to matter much in American foreign policy if a nation was a democracy or a dictatorship. What counted was whether a country was anti-communist or not, for America or against it. Besides, "democracy" must surely be one of the loosest political terms around, judging by the number of nations, from the benign to the tyrannical, which have adopted it as their own. What "democracy" seems to mean in the Israeli case is "friend."

Usually discourse analysis is more challenging. Take, for example, culture. For decades this concept, with its relativistic slant, appeared to reinforce the humanistic and egalitarian values of the discipline. It took a lot of hard thinking and imagination for the critique finally to emerge in which culture became associated with hierarchy, exploitation, and even racism.

But: As numerous writers have argued, discourse does not exhaust power, nor does a penetrating analysis necessarily negate patterns of privilege and advantage. Sheer political and economic forces in the global arena irreducible to discourse continue to call the tune. Even the move towards polyvocalism and dialogic approaches in ethnography inspired by the critique of anthropological authority has turned out to be largely window dressing. It might be added that in its sociolinguistic sense of examining power in language—for example, terms of address reflecting marital status or the switch from formal language to colloquialism when one turns from the boss to a buddy—discourse analysis is nothing new. What is novel, and important, is the text-power equation. As long as this version of discourse is not interpreted as the only form of power, it constitutes one of the rare analytic breakthroughs in recent social science.

13. *Power and resistance are twins.* For Foucault, power and resistance were more like twins than mere siblings. Wherever there was power there was resis-

tance; if resistance did not exist, neither did power; instead force was in operation.

But: Quite apart from the fact that resistance more often than not consists of minor protests that fail to redress inequality and domination, and tends to be romanticized, I question the usefulness of separating force from power. If this is done, power is to force as gender is to sexism and race relations are to racism. In other words, it becomes depoliticized, a conceptual approach which removes the sting from social relations. Of course, Foucault, Parsons, and Arendt are at perfect liberty to define power as they wish. But if they choose to exclude force from it, they are obligated to analyze force as a separate category; it cannot simply be ignored.

Something else should be said about resistance. Unlike discourse, it is an entirely commonplace idea. Russell referred to the safeguards that protect those subjected to power, and Galbraith (1983:72) observed: "resistance is as integral a part of the phenomenon of power as its exercise itself." Etzioni (1993:20), echoing Weber, wrote: "'power' means a generalized capacity to reduce resistance." In Wrong's words (1979:48): "power relations ... are never unilateral but always involve a minimal counter-influence exercised by the power subject on the power holder." Exactly the same message is found in the anthropological classic *African Political Systems*. As Fortes and Evans-Pritchard stated (1940:12): "the government of an African state consists in a balance between power and authority on the one side and obligation and responsibility on the other. ... A ruler's subjects are as fully aware of the duties he owes them as they are of the duties they owe to him, and are able to exert pressure to make him discharge these duties."

14. *Power and conflict are twins.* Several writers, including Bachrach and Baratz (1970:21), Dahl (1963:73), and Etzioni (1993:21) have observed that power and conflict are intrinsically connected, almost identical twins.

But: This may exaggerate the degree of strain in society, ignoring peace, pleasure, and amicable relationships, and overlook the possible positive aspects of power, such as the production of a memorable evening at the symphony, thanks partly to the mastery of the conductor. In a sense it also renders power expendable. If conflict always implies power, why bother with the latter term? The implication is that power is most useful in cases devoid of apparent conflict. A case in point might be feminist organizations, especially those which eschew a leadership structure in order to promote a sense of equality, where power contests sometimes emerge between heterosexuals and lesbians, higher class and lower class members, and white women and those of color.

15. *Power and culture are inimical.* Indeed, on the basis of the recent critique of culture, it might be concluded that metaphorically speaking power and culture constitute different species.

But: Eric Wolf certainly thought otherwise, and no doubt he did succeed in fusing power and culture in the sense of ideology. Moreover, if culture and power were not interdependent, discourse analysis would not make any sense, and ethnic and multicultural studies would be reduced to the shadows in the cave—charming folklore, native dress, and exotic cuisine.

16. *Power is an aphrodisiac.* Who needs Viagra when power is available? This is the stuff of novels, and occasionally of the local newspaper, and no doubt it has a basis in reality. Political conventions and elections seem to be charged with sexual electricity, even if people (maybe the majority) resist it. Nor is the political arena the only place it operates. The minister or priest, lit up by the power of the deity, occasionally has to fight off the moths—enamored members of the congregation. And to paraphrase Marx, a man may be ugly, but the power of money will transform him into Clark Gable or Rock Hudson.

But: For some people a mere sniff of power will turn their stomachs. Power-hungry individuals are regarded as lepers. Even people who have no particular grudge against authority figures may oppose differential power because of an idealistic commitment to equality, or at least an opposition to widespread inequality. Rather than elevating sexual passion, displays of power, at least for some people, stiffen class consciousness.

17. *Political resources (money, position, reputation) equal power.* This seems obvious. Surely the CEO of a large firm has more power than the janitor.

But: Several writers such as Bachrach and Baratz (1970:19) and Etzioni (1993:19) have insisted that there is an important distinction between the capacity to exercise power and its actual exercise. Dahl (1963:48 and 69) suggests that this is because a person may possess considerable resources but lack the skill to take advantage of them, or simply have no interest in doing so. Complicating the issue is the distinction between formal and informal power. When a political party, long out in the cold, suddenly and surprisingly finds itself elected to serve the people, it may rely excessively on the experience and advice of civil servants. Another obvious example concerns local politics, with economic elites behind the scenes making the important decisions, leaving the elected council to decide whether the cost of dog licenses should be raised.

18. *Power always brings change.* This seems to be implied in the conception of power as A's capacity to influence B despite B's resistance. Power involves decision-making. It is goal-oriented, active, dynamic. It makes things happen.

But: Power also can be used to impose stability, to sustain the status quo. As Dahl (1962:40) states, "influence is a *relation among actors* in which one actor induces other actors to act in some way they would not otherwise act. Of course this definition also includes instances in which actor A induces B to go on doing something he is now doing, though B would stop doing it except for A's inducements." Similar are the words of Etzioni (1993:18): "*Power is a capacity to overcome part of all of the resistance, to introduce changes in the face of opposition* (this includes sustaining a course of action or preserving a *status quo* that would otherwise have been discontinued or altered)."

19. *Power is the key concept in the social sciences.* It is not surprising that several famous political scientists such as Lasswell, Kaplan, and Morgenthau have defined their discipline as the study of power, but Bertrand Russell went a step further: power is the central concept in the social sciences in general.

But: Lukes (1986:4) remarked that power can't even be defined, and Champlin (1971:2) long ago referred to the disillusionment among political scientists about the importance of the concept. Numerous writers, McClelland (1971:64) and Wrong (1979:65) among them, have argued that power is so vague and meaningless that it should be discarded.

20. Power is the key explanation in the social sciences. I suppose that with a stretch of the imagination it could be claimed that because power is ubiquitous, an aspect of all social relationships, it is the key to explanation, despite being ill-defined; after all, multiple and contradictory definitions of basic concepts are the rule rather than the exception. Certainly the impression in anthropology in recent years is that power is the way forward, the basis of an explanation that will finally put our colonial past behind us.

But: Not everyone agrees that power is the key variable in human interaction. In an intriguing article, unfortunately unpublished, Eidlin contends that students of power have tended "to overestimate the role of power in society— to assume that everything that happens in society reflects the will of those in power or is the outcome of some kind of power struggle. In reality ... only a very small part of all that happens in any society ever comes up for deliberation or is consciously controlled or struggled over by anyone." Given Eidlin's argument, the expectation might be that he favors a structural perspective. That is not the case. Structural power, that residing in class, elites, or groups, is devoid of meaning in his judgment, and reified to boot. In contending that power plays only a minor role in society, Eidlin, a specialist on the former Soviet Union, flatly contradicts writers like Mann, Mills, and Galbraith who portray the population in contemporary Western societies as more controlled than at any time in previous history.

Eidlin's perspective contains two flaws. First, although he is no doubt correct that it makes little sense to attribute "will" or "aims" or "minds" to social groups and social structures, rather than to the individuals within them, it does not necessarily follow that the sheer weight and variation of the social structure fail to have an impact. Second, his perspective appears to hinge on the gap he had observed in the former Soviet Union between the decisions of leaders and the formal rules on the one hand and the widespread deviation from those decisions and rules on the ground level. Such a gap does not mean power is puny. It merely rediscovers what the transactional school of politics has argued all along: power unfolds primarily in the informal realm of social interaction.

There is, however, another objection to the idea that power is the key explanatory tool: *power can only be analyzed after the fact.* As Isaac has put it (1987:148): "The concept of power cannot function in any primary thesis for the basic reason that one can only analyze power by analyzing social relationships themselves." He continues: "The concept of power cannot furnish us with the key to the study of historical change because in order to analyze power we must undertake historically specific analyses." As Isaac concludes, "power is a purely formal concept, which has explanatory value only when attached to a theory of a historically specific social relationship or society. Outside of such a theory it is simply, in Marx's words, 'an abstract, eternal idea'."

Isaac is not the only writer to argue that power can only be analyzed after the fact. Half a century ago Bendix (1953) said much the same thing, and Etzioni (1993:19) more recently has observed that that is the major methodological objection to power. For those among us who have latched onto power as the savior of the discipline, Isaac's message should be sobering.

CONCLUSION

We are now in a position to offer several generalizations about power:

1. There is no more agreement in the literature about the nature or meaning of power than about any other major concept.

2. Except possibly for cases of explicit harmony, it doesn't add much to the analysis by merely stating that power is involved; power must be unpacked in order to render the analysis more nuanced and sensitive.

3. Power in the abstract is not fruitful for explanation, nor can it serve as a deductive model; power can only be analyzed in the context of human interaction—some would say after the fact.

4. A focus on power does not necessarily mean an opposition to inequality. For writers such as Parsons, and to some extent Foucault, power implies a conservative commitment. Any analysis that goes against the grain of popular thinking—in this case the contention that power is socially good—is, of course, intrinsically interesting. Yet in my judgment not only is power more often than not embedded in differential advantage, but when it is detected illegitimate behavior is exposed. For example, behind racism, rape, and incest we find power. We also discover one of the reasons that they escape censor: the victims of racism, rape, and incest often remain mute, ashamed to talk openly about their fates.

5. An understanding of power does not necessarily mean a rejection of power. Recently an individual told me that he sent his son off to university with a placard for the wall containing these words: "It's not what you know, nor who you know, but who knows you." To assure that his fatherly advice would be adhered to, he provided his son with a little notebook in which to record the names of influential contacts. Cynicism or hard-nosed reality? Take your pick.

6. The meaning of power is discipline-dependent; for psychologists it is a motive, for sociologists and anthropologists it is a relationship. Within a discipline, the meaning of power is paradigm-dependent; in sociology, Weberians regard power as voluntaristic, while Marxists favor the structural conception, even if, like Isaac, they make room for agency.

Actually, I object to the term *paradigm* being applied to anthropology because in my judgment the discipline has never got past the pre-paradigm stage. Even if we do employ the term, there is reason for doubting that it can be legitimately attached to the recent focus on power. Every new paradigm introduces a novel array of concepts. For example, the transactionalists, as they moved beyond structural functionalism, gave us terms such as arena, middlemen, factions, teams, and cores. Postmodernists introduced dialogic, polyvocal, trope, true fictions, tone, and text. The only really novel term in the recent literature on power that has had an impact is discourse, although Foucault's bio-power and disciplinary power also caught our interest. Hegemony and resistance have long been part of our vocabulary, and Bourdieu's habitus receives lip service but little serious attention. If a novel vocabulary is a meaningful measure of paradigmatic status, power falls short of the mark.

7. There is no ultimate evidence or logic to either support or reject the argument that power is the most basic human motive or the most basic socio-cultural variable. How could it ever be proven that power as a psychological motive is more fundamental than the drive for security, food, shelter, sex, happiness, hate, or companionship? It may be thought that the centrality of power in the socio-cultural realm is more apparent. When we inspect culture for power, we quickly spot ideology, when we examine social structure, we find stratification and its main components. To investigate power, in a sense we move closer to the surface where gender, class, race, and ideology operate. Yet how could we counter the argument that power is only a means to ends such as wealth and status, or that human interaction is characterized as much by generosity and shared pleasure as inequality?

8. Explanations in terms of culture often conceal underlying power as it flows through class, gender, race, and ideology. For example, a few years ago, I came across an article on gun control in the *International Herald Tribune* (March 14, 1996). It indicated that both in terms of the number of households with guns (almost 50 percent) and the number of murders by guns (15,546 in 1994) the United States is the dubious leader among industrialized nations. Proponents of gun registration and rigorous gun control could point to Japan for support. In that country only about one percent of households have guns, and only about 50 people are licensed to use handguns, which must be left at the firing range; not even the police are permitted to take their weapons home. Significantly, in 1995 only 32 murders by guns were reported.

However, if the comparative framework is extended to Switzerland, a different picture emerges. Like Japan, its murder rate by guns is very low. Yet at 27 percent of households it has one of the highest gun ownership rates in the industrialized world. In fact, the Swiss government actually issues machine guns and ammunition to its male citizens. This is because from their late teens until the age of 42 they serve in the militia. When their service is completed, they are at liberty to keep or sell their guns. Only in terms of handguns are Swiss laws restrictive.

The implication would appear to be obvious: culture is at play. Whether it be the strong bonds of community or values that emphasize the peaceful resolution of conflict, there appears to be something about "the way of life" in Switzerland that mitigates against interpersonal violence. The same thing might also account for the small number of deaths by guns in Japan, rather than their strict regulation. However, neither Switzerland nor Japan has a large dispossessed underclass. Moreover, gun-related deaths that do occur in these two countries are concentrated among those people who are poor and powerless. This would seem to add ammunition, so to speak, to the argument that gun-related violence reflects class issues rather than cultural ones. Instead of accepting that in the United States little can be done to cope with violence, except building bigger prisons, because it is ingrained in tradition, it would make sense to reduce the gulf between rich and poor; at least if a drop in the murder rate is a priority.

9. Not everything labelled culture can be reduced to power. Do heterosexual men hold hands in public, but not men and women? I well remember during my first months in Nigeria how long it took to get used to walking along a street hand in hand with male companions. Do lovers rub noses rather than kiss lips, whistle or clap to express displeasure, drive on the left side of the road rather than on the right? Do women as well as men habitually smoke pipes? These are examples of cultural variation, irreducible to power. While they may vary along class and ethnic lines, for the most part they require no further explanation than tradition. To the extent that they persist over the ages, they do so for two reasons. One is that they are relatively insignificant for political and economic forces (Steward's core). The other does bring power back into the picture: such expressions of cultural variation sometimes amount to resistance against global cultural hegemony.

Even in the above sense, however, "culture" can be ambiguous. For example, in February, 2000, I happened to turn on the television set as a football (or soccer) game for the African Cup between Nigeria and Cameroon was about to begin. The four referees shook hands, and two of them kissed each other on the cheek. It is hard to imagine that happening in the N.F.L. (National Football League). Yet it is equally difficult to make a case for culture in the old sense of a single people within a specific territory. While the practice of kissing cheeks may reflect culture contact and occur in societies where face-to-face relationships have not been obliterated by bureaucratic ones, it surely is not confined to any specific "culture" or nation-state.

One last example of ambiguity. A few years ago, while on holiday at a cottage in northern Ontario, friends from Montreal dropped by for a visit. At one point their two-year-old daughter squealed with delight as she watched a squirrel pivot around the top of a tall pine tree. Suddenly the squirrel tumbled into the air and landed by her feet, dead before it hit the ground. A man in the adjacent cottage, who was born and bred in the north, had plugged it with a .22 cartridge.

As we all attempted to placate the child, the discussion turned to the different cultures of the urban and rural settings. Yet even if the child had been capable of grasping the message, it would only have been half-true at best. One reason is that from the perspective of our neighbor, there was a rational purpose to his action: squirrels can wreak havoc if they get into a cottage. The other reason is that the man's actions did not necessarily reflect northern culture; not all northerners are hunters, nor would they all be so quick to dispose of a varmint with an enthralled child in the vicinity. As I have pointed out previously, when dealing with individual cases, personality must be entertained. As I got to know the man who pulled the trigger, I realized that although he was a charming raconteur, had he lived in the city he may well have been like the elderly man in one of Albert Camus's novels who found amusement in spitting on the cats that collected on the balcony below his own.

Chapter 5

Power and Ethnography

In this chapter the focus switches from the explanatory limits to the promises of power, which are explored in the context of ethnography. Although anthropology has changed considerably since World War II, the field work setting is still the ultimate test for our ideas, and hopefully it will help us sort out some of the debates raised in the previous chapters. The four case studies below are my own; they have been selected not because there is anything remarkable about them (although they certainly excited and challenged me), but because they are the ones I know best. They consist of a West African utopia which enjoyed enormous economic success, organized racism and anti-Semitism in Canada, violence in Corsica related to the vendetta era and the contemporary independence movement, and a peaceful village in rural Ontario that was kicked and coaxed along the path to modernity by invading city dwellers.

A WEST AFRICAN UTOPIA

In 1947, in the depths of the Niger Delta, a village that was destined to become famous in Nigeria and further abroad made its appearance. Bordering the Atlantic Ocean, and separated from the mainland by about 50 miles of mangrove swamp, Olowo, as I call the community, was established by several hundred Yoruba-speaking fishermen opposed to the killing of twins, a practice that had long disappeared from the Yoruba mainland, but still occurred in this remote region known as Ilaje. The opposition to twin killing had a political connotation. The Olugbo of Ugbo, who was the traditional *oba* (king) in Ilaje, controlled the practice and collected a fine from the parents of twins. Olowo people challenged his authority and interfered with his income, setting the course for major conflicts between them in the future.

During the wet season Ilaje was almost entirely flooded. Houses were built on stilts, and there were no roads, cars, or even bicycles. To get from one house to another meant using a canoe. Most men in Ilaje were subsistence fishermen. Women were responsible for smoking or drying the fish, which were then transported by canoe to the mainland and sold or traded for food staples such as rice and plantain.

Despite the inhospitable setting, within five years Olowo people had achieved remarkable economic progress. Sturdy wood-frame houses on stilts were constructed, rather than the thatch dwellings typical of the region, the furniture crafted by men skilled in carpentry. Olowo people also built a central boardwalk, making it possible to have bicycles and later a car for the leader, who assumed the traditional Yoruba title of *oba*. Twenty smaller boardwalks on either side of the main one connected all the houses. Before long there was a bakery, a shoe factory, a poultry farm, a small-engine repair shop, and a primary and secondary school. A large generator was purchased, providing the various industries and every house with electricity; eventually even an internal telephone system was put in place.

Although industries such as the shoe factory were not unimportant, the village's main sources of income were transportation and fishing. The carpenters, and others with a flair for technical work, built more than 20 large launches which carried passengers and produce throughout the Niger Delta, even penetrating into the neighboring country of Cameroon. It was not long before the community monopolized the transportation industry in the Delta, creating envy and hostility in the surrounding villages. Olowo people also began constructing small oceangoing fishing trawlers, relying on the firms from which they purchased the engines to provide the required expert assistance to install them. For the most part, however, the achievements of the villagers were their own. When four young men who had been sent to Europe for technical training returned to the community, they established a technical school; from then on even the advice of outside experts was expendable.

Olowo people, known as the Holy Apostles, explained their economic success in religious terms. It was a way to celebrate God and to demonstrate that they merited special attention; it also was a sign that they were blessed by God. The Holy Apostles considered themselves to be Christians. Most of them had previously belonged to the Cherubim and Seraphim branch of the *Aladuras,* one of the independent church movements in West Africa that had broken away from the mainstream Christian denominations introduced by missionaries.

Shortly after Olowo was founded, a major innovation was introduced: communalism. Money ceased being used within the village. There was no payment for work, all goods and possessions were held in common, and the profits from the various industries went to the central treasury. At this time an ascetic lifestyle prevailed. Women were not permitted to wear jewelry, nobody could have a watch, and only during ceremonial occasions did people wear shoes and dress in fine clothes, provided by funds from the treasury. The communal system also had a profound impact on social organization. The family, considered to be a rival to communalism, was suppressed, marriage was temporarily banned, and the village was divided along the central boardwalk into male and female sectors. Although marriage was re-established within a couple of years, taking the form of monogamy, husband and wife continued to live in separate houses in the male and female sectors, and children were not allowed to be raised by either their mother or their father. Communalism had a clear religious connotation in the village. It was modelled after the Biblical image of early Christian life. The man who introduced communalism, and many of the other innovations, apparently did so after receiving a vision from God. This was the village's leader or *oba*. In Yoruba society, an *oba* is a sacred leader, his roots traced back to the village of Ile-Ife where it was believed all life began. Although the *oba* in Olowo could not claim a genealogical connection to Ile-Ife, he certainly was regarded as a religious giant. His subjects thought he could communicate directly with the Deity, and while they loved and respected him, and obeyed his commands, they trembled in his presence. Such was the awe that he created that he might well be described as a charismatic leader. To do so, however, skims over the complex circumstances that gave rise to Olowo.

In the early 1940s, disaster struck the Ilaje region. Smallpox and cholera epidemics swept over the population, killing people off by the dozens. As Weber states (1971), for a charismatic leader to emerge, the soil must be hospitable to the seeds. With the death toll mounting, a number of prophets sprang up, some of them operating in healing houses, which were small huts built on stilts where the ill could be treated spiritually. At first the prophets restricted their efforts to warding off illness, and restoring those who had been attacked to good health. Since in Yoruba culture the main source of death was thought to be witchcraft, this meant nullifying, through prayer, the power of the witches. Eventually, however, a far more significant goal crystallized: immortality (*aileku*). The prophets began to claim that they could not only heal the afflicted, but even grant them immortal life—not in heaven, but on earth.

Immortality became the cornerstone belief of the Holy Apostles, and in 1945 an attempt was made to establish a village of the faithful near the present location of Olowo. The Olugbo of Ugbo, with the assistance of the colonial district officer, forced the Apostles to disband. The prophet who had led them at the time lost credibility—in Weber's terms he had not produced an appropriate sign of his charisma—and two years later it was another prophet, or rather prophets in the plural, who established Olowo. This was a period of intense political jockeying for leadership. The man who emerged as victor was certainly an awe-inspiring figure, but by no stretch of the imagination was he recognized by everyone as the obvious *oba* by virtue of his charisma. What he did manage to do was to physically force most of his competitors from the community. Several of these prophets soon founded their own villages, although none of them adopted the communal system, nor did they enjoy Olowo's spectacular economic growth. Four renowned prophets who remained in Olowo were manipulated by the *oba* so that their power was neutralized. He created the category of the four pillars, who became known as the deputy *obas*, effectively institutionalizing their authority at a notch below his own. The *oba* also established an elite organization called the Supreme Council of Elders, in this way co-opting prominent individuals who opposed him while rewarding those who supported him. With this last point in mind, it should be pointed out that one reason why this particular prophet emerged victorious was that more Olowo people originated from his natal Ilaje village than any other; they proved to be his natural supporters.

With the leadership issue settled, the socio-cultural character of the community began to take shape. Immortality, here on earth, was the dominant theme in the belief system. Its feasibility in the minds of the Apostles was reflected by the fact that they had neither a burial ceremony nor a burial ground. Because all Ilaje people were supposed to be buried in Ugbo, the traditional kingdom, with the Olugbo receiving payment for the privilege, immortality was another source of strain with the outside world. As a result of factors too complicated to explain here (see Barrett 1977), economic development soon became interpreted as a means to and sign of immortality. No wonder the Apostles were willing to work from daybreak to dusk with little personal material reward.

Despite the egalitarian thrust of communalism, a small but enormously powerful elite emerged, all of them men renowned for their spiritual gifts. They ruled the community with an iron hand. Ordinary members had no voice in whether they went to school, what house they lived in, what work they did, or whom they married. In order to leave the community simply to visit one of the nearby traditional villages, they had to get permission from the *oba*. Nonmembers were only allowed into the village during daylight hours. As time went by, people seemed to forget that there had been a bitter battle for the leadership in the early days of the community. Some of them remarked that even back then when the *oba* spoke in public he appeared to levitate, while others spoke in awe of a glow like a halo that seemed to surround his head—all of which suggest the manner in which charisma is manufactured after the fact.

During this period in the community's history, power took the form of force, manipulation, and ideology. Not only did the *oba* drive most of his competitors from the village, but in the succeeding years deviants were harshly punished. If they shirked community labor or attempted to defect, they were beaten severely with small sticks, and the hair on their head and genitals was shaved off to mark them as sinners. Manipulation was apparent in the creation of the category of four pillars. The main face of power, however, was probably ideologically conduced consent, or ideas fused to power in order to realize community goals set by the elite. With the *oba*'s promise of everlasting life on earth, it is understandable why people accepted the communal system, including the suppression of the family, and chased after economic success as if their lives depended on it—which from their perspective was literally true.

In 1963 the *oba* "travelled," a euphemism for death, although it was thought that he would return in the not too distant future. Up until then, the belief that nobody would die remained largely intact. This was partly because the actual death rate, according to some of my informants (or consultants, to be politically correct), was extraordinarily low. Another reason was that when a person "travelled," the lights were turned off, people were ordered to stay indoors, and the body was disposed of by a handful of men who had had that responsibility since the village's inception. Not only were almost all Olowo people prevented from witnessing what happened to the dead, but even to talk about them was taboo. When the *oba* passed away, however, adjustments to the concept of immortality no longer could be avoided. For a while it was preached that only the deserving would live in the village forever. By 1974, when I visited the Apostles for the third time, immortality was interpreted in conventional Christian terms as everlasting life in heaven for true believers.

The man who became the second *oba* was one of the prophets who had tried to become leader in 1947, and who had been named one of the four pillars. He immediately attempted to reverse almost all of his predecessor's innovations. Immortality remained the overwhelming goal, but rather than pursuing it via economic development, he emphasized direct worship. Under his reign, the economy faltered as people gathered on the main boardwalk singing hymns and chanting in "angel" language (*edo*), a form of speaking in tongues or glossolalia. The new leader, who became known as *Oba Aileku* (king immortality), banned marriage once again, as had been done when the village was first founded, and sought to discredit his predecessor's relatives. This was not an unusual move in Yoruba society. When a new *oba* assumes the throne, his relatives attempt to attach themselves to different lineages, because a kinship connection to the divine leader is considered a disadvantage.

Within a couple of years, the second *oba* suffered a major blow to his health which left him paralyzed. As some people stated, he was struck down by the holy spirit because of his attacks on the first *oba*'s memory and achievements. With the village in turmoil and nobody in charge, a man in his late 30s made his move. Although regarded as highly intelligent (he had been one of the young men who studied technology in Europe), he had never enjoyed the reputation as a religious individual, and indeed some members questioned his morals. Nevertheless, he began to circulate through the community singing hymns and announcing visions. He also portrayed himself as the first *oba* reincarnated, implying that the original leader indeed had returned, and occupied the young man's body (the routinization of charisma). After a few months he began to wear the crown, accepted the title of *oba*, and carefully consolidated his grip on the throne. Several of the elders had opposed him because they doubted his spiritual sincerity. The third *oba* easily manipulated them by showering them with gifts such as electric fans and even motorcycles. One of his first decisions was to reinstate marriage, only this time it took the form of polygyny. Women in the neighboring villages were energetically recruited, a new source of significant conflict between Olowo and the outside world; the majority who joined initially were given to the elders. Opposition also came from men in his own age bracket and lower, again because of doubts about his religious and moral character. The *oba* brought them on his side by giving them responsible leadership positions in the economy, and he created a new high status category specifically for them: the Faith and Work Council of Chiefs.

With his authority unchallenged, at least openly, he turned his attention to his major concern: the deteriorating economy. The village was a generation old, and people no longer seemed willing to work as hard as before for the collective good. The solution the *oba* came up with was revolutionary: capitalism. The communal system had been a cornerstone of the village's religious ideology, and the decision to ditch it merely confirmed the concerns of the elders. At first only a small percentage of the profits from the various industries was allowed to be claimed by the workers. By 1974 the transition from communalism to capitalism was virtually complete. At the same time the family re-emerged as a viable institution, initially among the elite, as wives (and their children) began to reside with their husbands.

With the introduction of private enterprise, the stratification system was transformed. During the communal era, there always had been a power elite, the members of which enjoyed high status and prestige but only minimal material advantages. With communalism gone, material rewards became legitimate, and the village began to be divided into rich and poor; this was even evident in residential patterns, as wealthy people built large houses in one sector of the village. Significantly, in almost every case the higher people's status during the communal era, the more probable they prospered after private enterprise emerged. This was largely because the elite had access to the treasury, and used funds from it to "purchase" community assets like the shoe factory, the bakery, and the boats.

The switch to private enterprise also transformed the social control system (see Barrett 1979), which actually went through three distinct phases: from normative control to repressive control and then back to normative again. During the first *oba*'s reign, when communalism existed, normative control was dominant. By normative control I mean the impact of beliefs, values, symbols, and norms on people's behavior. Obviously, there is a very close link, almost a tautology, between social control and power. What I have labelled normative control is equivalent to the type of power that was prominent during the village's early period: ideologically induced consent. The other two phases of social control occurred after private enterprise had been introduced. Although this momentous change did initially motivate people to work harder, it wasn't long before they began to demand all the profits, not just a small percentage, and they attempted to influence the *oba* by reducing their commitment to communal work. Resistance also was evident among the elderly, but from the opposite direction: for both religious and practical reasons, they agitated for a return to full-scale communalism, realizing that otherwise they were going to have to go back to work in order to feed themselves, or rely on the generosity of their relatives. Significantly, the majority of younger members who had attended secondary school sided with the elders; they openly criticized the *oba* for demolishing the exact feature of the village that had made it so special. The *oba*'s reaction was to lay down the law. People who opposed him were severely beaten, and their hair was shaved off. But that had always been done. What the *oba* did new was to establish several groups with specific social control duties, including monitoring the behavior of his subjects on a 24-hour basis and providing him with a written report each day. When it became clear to him that the educated youth were not going to be dissuaded from their protests, he expelled most of them from the community.

Only one sector of the population partly escaped physical punishment: women. Olowo men boasted that their female members were provided with freedoms and opportunities never enjoyed in Yoruba society. They could go to sea and fish, which was taboo for Ilaje women, and they toiled in the technical shop and repaired motors and bicycles. In other words, they could do the same work as men. However, almost never did a woman ride a bicycle, and in most cases they had fewer amenities, such as electric fans, than their husbands. At the same time they were punished less severely. According to Olowo men, this was because women lacked the capacity to appreciate their sins; thus punishment served little purpose. An alternative explanation, especially applicable to the new fe male recruits, is that had they been punished physically for disobedience or any other sin, they might have been more inclined to defect.

By 1974, roughly six years after private enterprise had been introduced, normative control had resurfaced. Even during the repressive stage, religious activity never disappeared, although it was restricted mainly to the Sunday church service. The third *oba* once said to me that if his subjects always behaved themselves, there would be no need even for the weekly service. Following the repressive stage, religious expression was encouraged, and people in white robes gathered along the central boardwalk to sing hymns. Members of the community also were granted new freedoms. Not only could they run their own businesses and keep all of the profits for themselves, but they also, for the first time since 1947, could leave and return to the village without anyone's permission. In other words, with the elite in control of the community's assets, it was in their interest to put freedom and liberalism for everyone on parade.

While the elite got its way in the end, and had enjoyed enormous power dating back to the days of the first *oba*'s reign, it would be a mistake to downplay the amount of resistance to it over the years. The third *oba* once explained to me that in order to lead he had to be continuously alert to what his subjects wanted, especially the influential elders renowned for their spiritual gifts. The obvious ways in which resistance was repelled by the three *obas* were force, manipulation, and authority joined to ideology. Less obvious, but no less effective, was discourse, especially that which related to "community." The term *community* summed up everything the Holy Apostles stood for: the path to everlasting life on earth, the defeat of sin, and spiritual and material superiority over their neighbors. Community also supposedly meant that everyone was equal, which in material terms was essentially true during the first *oba*'s reign. So powerful was the idea of community that if a man or woman disobeyed or decided to defect, he or she was thought to be morally compromised or even crazy, with the only hope of redemption being severe physical punishment, followed by arduous communal labor.

What is interesting is that after the initial turn to private enterprise, there was little apparent decrease in the amount of discourse devoted to community. Even as they took home a portion of the profits from their labors, and began to purchase their own clothes and bicycles, Olowo people continued to extol the virtues of communalism and egalitarianism. Without exception, this was done when visitors were in the village, but it was not restricted to such occasions. It was as if the hard reality of the world of capitalist struggle could be overcome or ignored by the consciousness of the past.

More surprising still, by 1974, when full-scale private enterprise had triumphed, discourse surrounding "community" had not entirely disappeared. Had it done so, members of the elite, by then wealthy as well as powerful, may have had to think twice before venturing out on the boardwalks, given the manner by which they had prospered. Of course, the third *oba* claimed, with considerable justification, that he had had no choice but to introduce private enterprise— the economy had begun to stagnate. Besides, a share in the profits was precisely what his subjects had demanded. What they had not counted on was the headstart enjoyed by the elite in adapting to the new economic order.

THE RADICAL RIGHT IN CANADA

"Hitler was a softy on the Jew question." These were the words of John Ross Taylor in 1978, the leader of the white supremacist and anti-Semitic Western Guard in Toronto, whose active participation in the far right began in the 1930s (Barrett 1987). A decade earlier, the first of four phases of organized far right activity in Canada took shape. In the 1920s the Ku Klux Klan had materialized in several provinces, including Saskatchewan, where it assisted the Conservatives in their successful attempt to overthrow the ruling Liberals. At that time the Klan was not only anti-Asian and anti-African, but also opposed to French Canadians and Catholics.

In the 1930s Fascism made its appearance on Canadian soil, converting Taylor into a true believer, and was especially pronounced in Quebec and Ontario. The National Social Christian Party in Quebec, led by Adrien Arcand, portrayed Hitler as the greatest man except Jesus Christ who had ever existed. In Ontario, there was a brownshirt party, and swastika clubs in different parts of the province. The outbreak of World War II put an end to the Fascist era, with Taylor and Arcand interned in a camp for the duration of hostilities.

The late 1940s and 1950s have been appropriately labelled the sanitary decades. Fascism, racism, and anti-Semitism were taboo topics, and those attracted to them were forced to keep a low profile. Then in the 1960s the first signs of a resurgent right wing made their appearance. This was the third phase, the two main organizations then being the Canadian Nazi Party and the Edmund Burke Society. The first organization brought Taylor back into the public spotlight, although he was not its leader. That honor went to John Beattie, who in later years reputedly became a police informer and switched from championing the swastika to the Union Jack in order to promote British racial supremacy. The Edmund Burke Society actually began as a highly conservative, anti-communist movement; not until later, by which time its name had changed to the Western Guard, did it openly embrace racism and anti-Semitism. This occurred during the 1970s, coinciding with the fourth phase of the Canadian radical right, when there was a virtual flood of new organizations, including the Ku Klux Klan again, the Nationalist Party, and the Aryan Nations.[1]

Although there were several planks in the far right's ideological platform, such as opposition to homosexuality and what it considered to be moral degeneration in general, the main one was the belief in the superiority of the white race, coupled to a great concern that white people were in danger of being wiped out by their enemies. These enemies included dark-skinned people, sometimes referred to as "the mud races." According to white supremacists, interracial mixing, or, as they preferred, mongrelization, was more dangerous to humankind than the atomic bomb, because without the genetic purity of "the master race" the world could not survive. Yet from the right wing perspective, the danger posed by people of color was nothing compared to Jews. It was Jews, bent on attaining world domination, so it was claimed, who manipulated blacks and whites to intermarry, and to kill each other off in racial battles. From the perspective of the far right, African-origin people were acceptable in their place, which meant not intruding into the white man's space except in a subservient role. Jews, in contrast, were considered dangerous vermin, a morally flawed "race" for which there was no place on earth.

Prior to the Enlightenment, racial persecution had been justified in religious terms; it was God's will; God had blessed the white race. With the advent of science, biology became the major source of ideological justification, giving rise to racial classifications based on phenotypes. In recent years, almost every scientific pronouncement that even remotely seemed to support a racial worldview has been gratefully latched onto by the radical right. Jensen and Rushton, psychologists who have claimed scientific evidence for racial superiority, have become heroes in right-wing circles. In the 1970s a regular weekly seminar was held by right-wing individuals in Toronto on the topic of sociobiology, which they interpreted as a blueprint for racial survival. Nevertheless, it would be an error to conclude that religion has ceased to be important among white supremacists. The attack on white people, they contend, is an attack on Christian civilization. Moreover, in recent decades a religious movement known as

Identity has emerged. Identity means just that—who white people are. The answer is God's chosen people. Identity has become a Christian umbrella organization for the far right, from members of the Ku Klux Klan to the Aryan Nations.

When ordinary citizens think of organizations like the Ku Klux Klan, their
minds probably turn to violence: the image of lynchings by hooded nightriders
in the southern United States in the past. Power in these organizations today
still takes the form of force, although on the Canadian scene force plays a greater
role in discourse—diatribes about what is in store for the enemy—than in actual physical confrontation. While occasionally individuals are beaten merely
because of the color of their skin, most incidences of violence involve clashes between the far right and the far left, and sometimes with Jewish groups. It could
even be argued that far more violence occurs *within* the right wing rather than
with its ideological opponents. The degree of rivalry and petty jealousy among
racists and anti-Semites was astounding. One reason was the Führer principle.
Leaders of the various organizations, aspiring to be the top dog, lashed out at
each other; the cult of personality often overwhelmed ideology and beliefs, which
did not differ greatly from one organization to another. Ironically, ethnic prejudice sometimes was the source of enmity. One man contended that he was superior to anybody else in his organization because he originated from the part
of Holland supposedly inhabited by the purest Aryans. A person with a Slavic
background was regarded as morally flawed because of his genetic history. Class
differences, too, played a role. Two leaders in the movement were at each other's
throats because of class snobbery traced back to their different origins in Germany. A less concrete, but nevertheless significant, source of strain within the
radical right was its worldview. Practicing the politics of separation, latching on
to what for all intents and purposes were pan-human weaknesses such as ethnocentrism and xenophobia in order to build a political philosophy, members of
the far right were programmed to see the worst in each other.

Sometimes the confrontations shifted from words to deeds. For example, a
Klansman who had fallen out of favor struck back by slitting the throats of two
dogs doted on by the Klan leader. The latter retaliated by putting out a contract
on the other's life, but it turned out that the man he had hired to do the job was
an undercover police agent. Around the same time the Klan leader became involved in a plot to overthrow the country of Dominica, the long-range plan being
to establish a haven and base of operation for the far right. The Klan leader was
charged on conspiracy to commit murder and to overthrow a foreign government (as well as various forgery schemes), and ended up in jail. Two things are
significant about this turn of events. First, only rarely were members of the far
right brought to court on the basis of their racist beliefs and action; instead, it
was various types of conventional illegal behavior that got them in trouble. Second, among the tactics employed to confront organizations like the Western
Guard and the Ku Klux Klan, the most decisive and effective was the sheer application of force by the police, aided by their intelligence divisions.

Force, then, was certainly not a thing of the past in the radical right, but it played second fiddle to ideology and manipulation. Ideology, power fused to ideas in order to promote vested interests, often took the more narrow shape of propaganda. Ernst Zundel, for example, an immigrant from Germany, devoted his adult life to creating and distributing documentary evidence that the Holocaust was a hoax. Some of his competitors within the radical right accused him of promoting Jewish interests: by loudly denying the Holocaust, he was helping to maintain its high profile. This bring us to the question of tactics in the right wing. Decisions had to be made whether to remain underground and attempt surreptitiously to influence public opinion and events; or go public and even contest elections, while recognizing that the chances of winning were remote, but motivated by the media coverage that ensued; or paint one's organization in moderate colors, even if it did covertly embrace racism, anti-Semitism, and violence, the assumption being that the Canadian public was not ready yet for a full-blown radical right party.

Those committed to resisting organized racism and anti-Semitism had a comparable challenge. Should these organizations be legally banned, or would that drive them underground, making it more difficult to monitor them? Should they be opposed at all, especially by the media, or does that just provide them with free advertising? One thing was certain: there was a symbiotic relationship between the far right and the media. Organizations such as the Ku Klux Klan relied on the media to raise their public profile, the media fed on the inherent sensationalism to hook an audience. Having said all this, it must also be pointed out that without media coverage, opposition to the radical right might be much slower to build. Right-wing leaders, incidentally, were perfectly aware that they could only manipulate the media for so long; eventually the discourse would shift clearly to an anti-Fascist stance. Even negative coverage, however, sometimes was welcomed in the far right; at least somebody was taking it seriously. Indeed more than one leader complained that there was a conspiracy in the media to ignore them. That was occasionally true. Sophisticated opponents of neo-Fascism took the position that the most effective way of handling far right organizations, at least if they were merely preaching to the already converted, was the insulation technique—actively making sure, especially by overtures to the media, that their low profiles remained that way.

In the early 1980s, James Alexander McQuirter, the leader of the main Ku Klux Klan organization in Canada, made a pitch for what he labelled positive racism. The modern Klansman, he announced, wore a suit and tie, not a hooded white robe. The Klan was not opposed to anyone on the basis of skin color or religion; if a prospective member expressed racial hatred, McQuirter claimed, he or she was shown the door. The white race was not necessarily the smartest on earth; it was merely different, albeit unusually endowed with moral principles and a capacity for civilization. The Klan eschewed violence, and hoped for nothing less than amicable relationships among the world's several races, each with its own unique strengths and each in its own territory. At least that was the image of the Klan promoted publicly—an apt example of manipulation via discourse.

Anti-racists had their own discourse. Members of the Ku Klux Klan and similar organizations were evil incarnate, ogres, devils with horns passing themselves off as human beings. Such a viewpoint no doubt firmed up the opposition to the far right, but it was not completely accurate. Some members of the far right held responsible jobs, and by all measurements except one—their racist inclination—would be regarded as people of high moral principles. It is understandable why the image of the ogre was more palatable to anti-racists. If ordinary, average citizens could be racists and anti-Semites, that meant one's neighbor and one's fellow worker might be one of them—indeed, the entire society was potentially implicated.

Often manipulation was less subtle than the discourse concerning positive racism. For example, a Klansman in British Columbia sent a letter to McQuirter crowing that he had done it again: sucked in the media, which could hardly wait for his impending visit to Vancouver. There also was a policy in the Ku Klux Klan and some of the other organizations to infiltrate left-wing groups, especially in the university setting (of course, the converse happened as well). On one occasion McQuirter advised me to fire my research assistant, a former student doing graduate work at the time at a Canadian university. As the Klan leader explained, one of his members had joined a Marxist group on the campus, and discovered that my assistant was an active member.

I have not said much about stratification here because its principal component—race—is obvious. Class and gender, however, also played their parts. The membership of most of the main organizations was divided into three sections. At the top were the leaders, with public profiles, many of them well-educated. A second section consisted of younger members, usually with minimal formal education, who led the charge when a physical confrontation with left-wing groups erupted, and carried out some of the dirty tricks such as painting swastikas on synagogues. Then there was the silent membership. These were people who embraced the neo-Fascist ideology, but not openly, and were an important source of financial support, both in terms of membership fees and ad hoc contributions. This section, like the leadership, was relatively well-educated and essentially middle class, although it did include some high placed professional people.

As for gender, it will come as little surprise that the ideal woman was a housewife, happy in her husband's shadow. It sometimes was said that women were the weakest link in the white race's chain. This was partly because they were thought to be more vulnerable than men to race-mixing, and partly because their lack of commitment to the cause held their spouses back. There was, however, a woman's organization within the Klan in the past (Kamelia), and in recent years the women's movement has even penetrated the radical right. More than ever before, women have begun to demand leadership roles. For example, in the 1980s, after McQuirter was tossed in jail, Ann Farmer (not her real name), who was a university student at the time, attempted to replace him as leader. By then, however, the Ku Klux Klan in Canada was in disarray, and that fact, along with considerable opposition from male members, thwarted her ambition to become a nationally accepted leader.

If conflict and power are twins, conflict, power, and racism must be triplets. Just as it does not add much in situations of pronounced conflict to observe that power is involved, the same is true for racial contests. In the far right, power is manifested in force and manipulation, supplemented by discourse and the cult of the personality. On the Canadian scene, force is more likely to be part of the discourse rather than acted out in behavior, except for clashes between members of the right wing themselves. Force is conveyed even in part of the vocabulary of the far right—words such as swastika, and the Ku Klux Klan label. McQuirter once stated that he established his branch of the Ku Klux Klan in Canada for a simple reason: its sensationalism. Before doing so, he had been largely ignored.

Prospective members of the far right were exposed to a massive racist and anti-Semitic literature, including in-house publications, and regular group discussions helped them to see the light. This might be interpreted as persuasion, although in this context persuasion blurs into manipulation and propaganda-cum-ideology. At the stage when the media were ripe for exploitation, far right organizations sometimes attempted to influence public opinion, but rarely did the leaders see much advantage in attempting to persuade outsiders that race counted for everything, and that there was a Jewish conspiracy to eliminate white people. Even Zundel's efforts to discredit the Holocaust were often mocked by his fellow travellers. The assumption was that the vast majority of Canadians were incapable of hearing the message because of left-liberal brainwashing. Only when society finally exploded, which was believed to be inevitable, would white people wake up to the reality of racial dynamics. In the meantime, the leaders of the far right saw their job as making sure that Fascism had a committed fighting force ready and prepared for the battle ahead.

Power is pertinent here in a context not yet considered—the impact of American society on Canadian society, including racial matters. As each new phase of the Ku Klux Klan emerged in the United States, it was not long before it penetrated Canada, with the exception of the Klan's initial establishment in the 1860s. McQuirter's "positive racism" was copied directly from David Duke, a prominent far right member in America. At one point McQuirter even flirted with the idea of establishing a branch of Duke's NAAWP (National Association for the Advancement of White People) in Canada, as a counterbalance to the NAACP (National Association for the Advancement of Colored People). Former Prime Minister Pierre Trudeau once quipped that living next to the United States was like sleeping alongside an elephant. When the elephant twitched, Canadians jumped. Now that is power. Yet it would be a mistake to think that everything that smacks of racism in Canada, including the far right variety, is an American virus that unfortunately slipped over the border. From the treatment of its

Aboriginal population to Asian and Caribbean migrant workers, Canadian intolerance has required no instruction from Americans.

Canadians, in their ethnocentrism, often pride themselves for being a kinder,
gentler people than their neighbors to the south—more tolerant, more obedient and respectful of authority; in short more "civilized." Although the only
solid difference may in fact be Canada's relative lack of power on the world stage,
even if the above differences did once exist, it is improbable that they will continue in the future, primarily as a result of NAFTA and the evaporation of a pro-
tective Canadian nationalism. As Canadian institutions and values become increasingly like those in America, and the gap between the rich and poor widens
and social programs are decimated, we can make an unwanted prediction: race
relations will increasingly resemble those in the United States.

CORSICA: LAND OF BEAUTY AND VIOLENCE

The image of Corsica was in my head: the scent of herbs and flowers in the
spring, the sweep of the beaches, the chestnut trees on the mountain plateaus,
succulent salamis, smoked eels and blood sausage; and of course the people, the
stain of the vendetta in their veins. The man sitting across from me was slicing
slivers of sheep cheese, which we were washing down with strong red wine. His
wife and daughter were hovering around the table, quick to bring more cheese
from the small refrigerator and later a cake with no icing. The scene was pleas-
ing and ever so familiar: a solid peasant family, the fare simple and delicious, the
mood warm and hospitable.

However, this was not a Corsican family, and certainly I was not nestled on
an island in the Mediterranean. Instead I had been invited into a small apart-
ment in Paris inhabited by a Portuguese family in charge of the maintenance of
a large student residence. Why, then, the uncanny feeling of being in Corsica?
What I had sensed, I think, was social class. The Portuguese family did not remind me of the doctors, lawyers, and wealthy entrepreneurs whom I had met in
Corsica. Instead it was the shepherd in the valley and the shopkeeper in the village.

I have begun in this rather fanciful manner for a couple of reasons. One is to
drive home the point that culture is often confused with class. No doubt it is reasonable to suggest that connected to each class level is at least a loose set of values, attitudes, and behavior, but these don't add up to culture in the form of a
nation, nor are they restricted in space to a single geographical locality. Another
reason is to nip in the bud any notion that Corsica constitutes a homogeneous,
unique culture. Not only are class divisions salient, but ethnic ones too, and if
ever the assumption were applicable that culture is a process, as Boasian diffu-
sionism suggests, rather than a finished product or thing, Corsica fits the bill.
For virtually all of its known history it has been plundered and colonized by external powers (Pomponi 1979). There were Greek settlements as early as 500

BC, followed by Saracens, Moors, Romans, and Pisans, to name only a few of the invaders. By the fourteenth century the Genoese controlled the island, finally vacating it to the French in the latter part of the 1800s. Even the British briefly laid claim to the island, betraying the man who had invited them there to help Corsica achieve independence. This was Pascal Paoli, a greater hero to Corsicans than their more famous native son, Napoleon.

No doubt the Isle of Beauty, as Corsica often is called, was a jewel in France's crown, but in the late 1800s the vendetta, or family feud, was still in full swing. By the early part of the twentieth century the vendetta had pretty well petered out, but that did not mean the end of violence. Stepping into the vacuum was a muscular independence movement which in recent years has reached a level of violence next to which the vendetta has been said to resemble a tea party.

THE VENDETTA ERA

Three Corsican axioms capture the vendetta mentality: revenge is a dish best served cold; murder is the ultimate expression of power; blood is not for sale—nothing, money or otherwise, can compensate for the assassination of one's family member except the counter-death of the murderer or one of his close relatives.

In a population at the height of the vendetta of around 110,000, about one person in every 100 died in family feuds. As it was sometimes said, Corsicans killed more readily than they stole (Busquet 1920, Wilson 1988). The most trivial incident could set off a vendetta—kicking a dog, an insult in public, and especially any gesture or act that remotely questioned a woman's honor. Touching a woman's hair in public, known as l'attacar (symbolic rape), immediately led to enmity. The vendetta unit was the extended family. A man with several brothers, who could be rallied in a crisis, was an attractive marriage partner. There was a Corsican saying that three sons were wanted for every daughter, again partly so the fighting force would be strong.

While honor and dishonor were at the surface of the vendetta syndrome, there was nothing honorable about the circumstances of assassination. If you could ambush a person and plug him with a bullet or stick a knife in him when his back was turned, that was the thing to do. If the person had just left his mistress, meaning that his soul would go straight to hell, so much the better. There were, however, implicit rules connected to the vendetta. If a person of high status, such as a medical doctor, was assassinated, his family had a recognized right to kill two people in the other family. Priests, women, the elderly, and strangers were supposed to be non-belligerents and off-limits. Yet that was not always the case. Lay priests were fair game, and in a village in the mountains where I lived for several months, a local priest in the previous century stepped out of the church and shot a member of the congregation whose family had been locked in battle with his own. The priest fled to the maquis (the dense bushes that covered the mountain slopes), becoming a bandit of honor, a term of respect then in Corsica (Marcaggi 1978).

As for women, there was a time when they were considered too insignificant to be killed. Curiously, an index of the improving status of Corsican women was that eventually it was not dishonorable to take their lives, at least as second-best targets when their fathers or brothers weren't available. Women also played a major role in the vendetta. More so than men, they kept the goal of vengeance alive. When a family member was murdered, the women preserved the bloody garments and raised their male children to seek revenge, even if it took two or three generations to do so. This probably explains why vengeance was thought to be inherited and interminable, and why women were thought to have had an even greater craving for it than did men.

Women also sometimes carried out vengeance themselves. In one case a woman made her way to the house of a man who had seduced and jilted her, and finding nobody home except a boy, shot him dead. In another case, a woman whose husband had taken a mistress waited until he fell asleep after they had copulated and then drove an axe through his head. She was sentenced to 10 years in prison, considered to be very severe for a crime of passion. At that time, for example, a man who had murdered his adulteress wife was fined only 10 francs. Even if a woman was raped, the consequences were not necessarily limited to hunting down and killing the perpetrator. She was considered irrevocably damaged, and her own family might kill her, usually by poison.

While force obviously was the dominant face of power during the vendetta era, sometimes it was augmented by manipulation. For example, two people in love who were denied the right to marriage by their families would enact *l'attacar*; their families would have no choice but to consent to the marriage if a feud was to be avoided. This technique was sometimes resorted to in order to circumvent an arranged marriage, the prevalent form at the time. Feuds were fought over honor on the surface, for apparently the most trivial reasons, but underneath the motivation often was the prospect of material advantage. For example, a large landowner, with a covetous eye on his neighbor's property, might intentionally initiate hostilities. Under the cover of vendetta, he would destroy his neighbor and take over his land. Similarly, an ambitious young man might seduce a woman of higher status. Her parents would have no option but to agree to marriage, unless they were prepared to kill her and launch a vendetta against the seducer and his family. Since there was little material advantage or honor in fighting an inferior, the seducer's gamble sometimes paid off.

To move beyond the obvious—that power, in the form of force, was intrinsic to the vendetta—we must try to understand why the vendetta existed in Corsica, and in other places such as Albania (Boehm 1984, Durham 1928, Hasluck 1954). Corsican popular literature contains some rather fanciful explanations. One is that it was in their blood, implanted there as a result of intermarriage with North African invaders centuries ago. Another is that it was an expression of a nervous condition brought on by malaria, which was endemic along the island's east coast until the American military eradicated it by DDT after World War II. Sometimes the argument has been that Corsicans simply love firearms, or that the *maquis* offers a ready refuge should they be inclined toward violent acts. Then there is the assertion that the vendetta was a Genoese import. It is correct that the family feud thrived among the Genoese, but this argument is confounded by a simple fact: the vendetta existed in Corsica prior to the Genoese occupation.

Somewhat more sophisticated is the suggestion that the vendetta was an expression of resistance to Genoese rule. The fact that Corsicans were attacking each other does not negate this possibility, because it is commonplace for colonized people to turn their frustrations against themselves. Certainly there is some evidence that the bandits were occasionally politically conscious, motivated by a hatred of the occupying force. When the French took over Corsica there was a sharp upsurge in the vendetta rate, suggesting a political link. It also has been argued that the vendetta was encouraged by the Genoese, a sort of divide-and-rule policy played out with human life.

The long Genoese occupation was harsh and ruthless, denying justice to Corsicans and fragmenting their society. This leads to another plausible explanation. The vendetta emerged as a form of self-help, somewhat akin to the role of violence in the early American West. In other words, it constituted a covert system of justice which helped to regulate the society. When this argument is tied to the suggestion that, like the Sicilian mafia, the vendetta in Corsica made its appearance at a time when feudalism was on the way out, but capitalism was still not fully developed, thus creating a political vacuum, it makes even more sense. In this connection, it should be pointed out that the clan system was one of the political entities that stepped into the vacuum. Based on ties of kinship and patron-client links, the clan flourished in the informal realm of politics, its inherent self-interest thwarting the emerging state, but rendering life somewhat more patterned and predictable than it otherwise might have been. This last point has been elevated by Black-Michaud (1975) to one of the key explanations of blood feuds. His argument is that feuding societies are essentially amorphous, with little to hold them together. Feud constitutes a social relationship and a system of communications, resulting in a degree of societal cohesion that otherwise would not exist.

Both ecology and social structure seemed to have some impact on the vendetta rate, although it would be an exaggeration to portray them as the key factors. The vendetta was more prevalent in the isolated mountainous regions of southwest Corsica where feudalism persisted than in the plains on the east coast and the north where commerce had been most developed. Then, too, there was the potential influence of consanguinity. Cousin marriage was much more widespread in Corsica than on the French mainland; the underlying assumption was that there was less risk in bringing a relative rather than a stranger into the family bosom. This may be relevant because of the commonplace anthropological assumption that marriage beyond blood relatives—affinal marriage—is necessary to integrate society. If people married only consanguines, society would be reduced to war against all on the basis of biological consciousness and organization.

Ecology and social structure also figure prominently in the literature on warfare and feud. Primitive warfare is often portrayed (Harris 1975) as a mechanism to bring the population size in harmony with its ecological capacity. Because Corsica was quite underpopulated, especially in comparison to Sardinia and Sicily, this explanation doesn't seem to fit. However, it should be pointed out that much of the land in Corsica was too rocky or remote to be cultivated, and the less cultivation the more prevalent the vendetta.

As for social structure, the conventional argument is that warfare involves an entire sociopolitical unit such as a tribe or state against another, while feud involves part of such a unit against another part. Some writers such as Peters (1967) have claimed that feud can only exist when the units of social organization within a society are discrete, with no criss-crossing ties of loyalty. Yet this makes no sense in the Corsican case. One extended family pitted against another certainly was the structural basis of the vendetta. But not only did feuding individuals sometimes switch sides, but there was a considerable amount of killing *within* the extended family, especially between brothers. The position taken by Peters seems to be another example in which social structure is exaggerated at the expense of individual variation and inconsistency.

By the twentieth century, the vendetta, and the banditry associated with it, had almost disappeared. This was partly the result of massive force employed by the French state. Laws against carrying arms were enacted, and the murderer's house sometimes was destroyed, with salt dumped on his land. Even a fugitive's relatives suffered. They had to pay the costs involved by the pursuing police, and occasionally their properties were levelled as well. An all-out effort to rid the island of bandits was launched by the French, with a mobile force of soldiers put together for that purpose. There was an interesting expression employed then by the police: *tué par les gendarmes huit heures après sa mort* (killed by the police eight hours after his death). Sometimes a fugitive had already been murdered by his enemies before the police tracked him down. When that occurred, their practice was to shoot into the corpse—an unusual demonstration of power, to say the least.

The sheer force employed by the French state no doubt had an impact. Yet what really reduced the vendetta and banditry to historical memory was simply social change. As the legal system and social structures of the French state penetrated Corsican society, and capitalism displaced feudalism, individualism and social mobility eroded the family solidarity on which the vendetta depended.

THE CONTEMPORARY INDEPENDENCE MOVEMENT

In the early 1990s my wife and I, having just arrived back in Corsica, were strolling down the main street of a small town, enjoying the balmy September evening. All of a sudden I felt a blast of wind whipping over my face, and then came the sound of an explosion. A bomb, not a large one, had just gone off in front of a grocery store on the other side of the street.

A couple of weekends later we joined several Corsican friends under the chestnut trees which bordered a mountain stream, the green valley stretched out below us. We had been invited for a simple lunch, but the meal, course after course, had (typically) gone on for the entire afternoon. Our good-natured host, who had been born in a village a couple of miles farther up the mountain, was obviously pleased to share the quintessential Corsican experience: the gathering of friends and family in a dream-like setting of peace and beauty.

These are the two faces of contemporary Corsica: bombs going off on a regular basis, but people getting on with their lives, going to work as usual, raising their families, gathering at the cafés to sip pastis and play cards, drawing as much pleasure from life as human beings elsewhere.

When the explosion occurred next to the grocery store, nobody appeared to be very concerned. After all, at least 500 bombs per year go off on the island. The police station was only a short distance away. Usually the gendarmes are everywhere, a clutch of them staring at you over their machine guns after your vehicle has been stopped on a country road. On this occasion, however, it was at least a half-hour before two gendarmes drove up in their blue Renault 4. Rather than rushing to the scene of the crime, they stopped to shake hands and kiss friends on the cheek. People gathered along the street were upset because of the inconsiderate manner in which the bombing occurred. The person responsible, they stated, should have placed it inside the store and timed it to explode in the middle of the night, rather than exposing innocent bystanders to injury (only one man had been hurt). But they did not assume that the bomber had acted without reason. Maybe, it was said, there had been a history of hostility between the bomber and the storeowner's family. Or perhaps he or she had been shortchanged, and was merely getting even. Then there was the fact that the owner of the store was not a Corsican, but an immigrant from Italy.

In that same small town over the next few months, the local school was set on fire, a waiter in the process of serving fish soup was gunned down, and the town's only supermarket was levelled—the enormous blast bringing us wide awake in the middle of the night. The sound of guns going off did not necessarily mean somebody had been killed. Even when there was reason to celebrate, such as the victory of a Corsican football team, people took to the streets, pistols and rifles blazing. On one such occasion, while I dined with a friend, he pointed his rifle out the window and blasted away at the town clock. Getting into the spirit of things (so to speak), I took a few shots myself.

The sources of violence were several: personal enmities, election squabbles, drug-running, and domestic problems. Yet the main one was connected to the goal of political independence. There was nothing new about the search for independence. That had been the driving force behind Paoli's career in the mid-1700s, and in the 1920s there was an autonomist organization called *Partitu*

Corsu D'Azione. In the 1960s, however, the independence movement literally took off. What sparked it was the settlement in Corsica of about 17,000 *pied noir,* French citizens who had been forced to flee from Algeria after its own successful bid for independence. The *pied noir,* unfairly backed financially by the French government, many Corsicans claimed, quickly revolutionized industry on the island and became its dominant force. Corsican nationalists had always complained that the French government had tried to manipulate them by encouraging outsiders to emigrate to the island and Corsicans to leave it, and the facts supported them. In the nineteenth century more than 100,000 Italians settled in Corsica, while Marseilles eventually became home to twice as many Corsicans as remained on the island.

Soon after the *pied noir* invasion, two independence organizations made their appearance. For the most part they attacked property rather than people, blowing up state-owned buildings such as post offices. More frivolously, virtually every road sign on the island was shot through with holes, and the initials of independence organizations sprayed on. It was not until the late 1990s, when signs were written in both French and Corse (the indigenous language), that the practice was partially (not entirely) abandoned.

Due to a tragic confrontation resulting in death between the gendarmes and ARC (the leading autonomist organization at the time), the movement faltered in the mid-1970s (see Simeoni 1975). By the 1980s the search for autonomy or independence was back on track, with a new organization seeming to emerge on an annual basis. Some of these organizations had the goal of independence (such as FLNC), others only autonomy (for example, MPA). Most of the organizations were clandestine, but like the IRA's Sinn Fein in Northern Ireland, there usually was an overt political wing. Significantly, there also was an anti-autonomous and anti-independence movement in Corsica (for example, FRANCIA), manned by people who were determined to keep Corsica within the French state. Occasionally, they could play as rough as the independence groups.[2]

In the 1990s, with yet more organizations mushrooming, violence reached a new level and took a different direction. The number of bombings multiplied, the targets were sometimes located on the French mainland, and not just property but people too came under attack. At the same time rivalry among the various clandestine groups turned ugly. In vendetta-like fashion, they began to kill each other off. By the early 1990s there were around 30–40 politically motivated murders of Corsicans annually, few of them ever settled in court. The extent of violence had reached such a height that it drove a previously dormant section of society to action: women.

As in the vendetta era, Corsican women in the 1980s and 1990s were not totally inactive in the independence movement, although their main contribution was to provide assistance to their fugitive brothers and husbands. That all changed, but in a completely different direction, in January, 1995. In Bastia and Ajaccio, Corsica's two largest cities, peace rallies were organized by women. Calling themselves *Les Femmes du Manifeste pour la Vie,* hundreds of women—

within months, thousands—signed a petition calling for the end of violence on the island. Before the year was out, another group named *Femmes Contre la Violence en Corse* had splintered away from *Manifeste pour la Vie*. One reason was that the first group of women eventually allowed men to join the organization. The members of *Femmes Contre la Violence* also embraced a broader set of goals: women's rights, and an anti-racist program.

Back in the 1980s a comparable movement for peace had been initiated by Corsicans who supported continuing ties with France, and a short-lived women's group, with a feminist agenda, called *Donni Corse* (Corsican Women) had existed. But there had never been anything like *Manifeste pour la Vie* and *Femmes Contre la Violence*, either in terms of the sheer numbers involved or the impact on Corsican consciousness. In view of the expectation that women should remain in the shadows of men, their decision to openly petition for peace was courageous. In fact, the names of those who signed the petition initially were printed in Corsican newspapers. The members of the various independence organizations clearly were not amused. Their interpretation was that the efforts of women were simply playing into the hands of the French state. Whether or not the women's peace efforts will have any greater success in the long run than those initiated by women in Northern Ireland is probably too early to say, but the odds against it are staggering.

The Corsican independence movement faces some familiar obstacles. Like all nationalistic movements, its belief is that nation and state should be a single entity. But in a multi-ethnic society, what constitutes a nation? How is it possible to talk in terms of "a people" without excluding parts of the population, thus inviting the racist label? Some Corsican nationalists have countered that it doesn't matter what a person's ethnicity or religion is. All that counts is whether a person "feels" Corsican and is committed to its liberation.

Another problem is that not everybody wants independence, perhaps especially people drawing salaries from state enterprises, the elderly, and women. Corsican activists have charged the French state of deliberately manipulating the first two categories to its side by providing seductive subventions and pensions. As for women, it appears to be the case that they perceive less benefit in an independent Corsica than do men. Under French rule women have enjoyed a degree of autonomy and economic prospects unknown to them in earlier times. Their worry is that an independent Corsica might see them once again under the thumbs of their fathers and husbands.

The independence movement has divided Corsican people, possibly not quite down the center, because it appears that those in favor may be a minority. A vivid illustration of the division is reflected in recent books written by two Corsicans, both of them former reporters for the daily newspaper, *Nice-Matin*. Bourdiec (1996), an avid proponent of independence, attributes all of Corsica's problems to the French government. It is the state-controlled discourse, he contends, that has savaged the image of the nationalists, and to some degree of Corsican people in general. The Corsican "problem" is portrayed as irrational, the works of crazed individuals operating like the Mafia. Just as it was possible that the Ge-noese encouraged the vendetta in order to weaken Corsican opposition, this au-thor suggests that the French state has implicitly encouraged the recent trend in which members of the various clandestine organizations murder each other. Bourdiec especially laments the disappearance of the Corsican language, and forecasts that in an independent Corsica, Corse will become the language of ev-eryday life, with English rather than French as the second language taught in the schools.

The message in Giudici's book (1997) could hardly be more different. Cor-sica, he argues, was just as well-positioned as the Côte d'Azur in southern France for an economic takeoff. The fact that it stagnated instead is, according to the author, the fault of Corsican people alone. His argument is that Corsica is stuck in a mentality that rewards power rather than production. Everything is per-sonalized and politicized, including economic exchanges. The clans systemati-cally subvert the legal system, made possible in part by *omerta*. This is the code of silence. In the vendetta era it very definitely operated. For example, a 10-year-old boy who had been persuaded by gendarmes to reveal the hiding place of some fugitives paid the ultimate price: killed by his own father. *Omerta*, I can attest, was very much alive in the 1990s. On one occasion I had spent a lazy afternoon with an elderly shepherd. He was in good spirits, and all seemed well. The next day I read in the newspaper that a body had been found near his house shortly after my visit. When I later questioned him about the matter, he gave the stock answer: he heard nothing, saw nothing, and made it perfectly clear that the sub-ject was closed.

The great German sociologist, Max Weber, once spent a holiday in Corsica, which makes it appropriate to conclude with his perspective on power. It would be difficult to come up with a more apt example of the capacity of one person to influence another despite resistance than the vendetta. As the Corsican saying puts it, murder is the ultimate expression of power. However, if the vendetta to some degree was a rebellion against foreign control, it cannot be said that resis-tance was efficacious; after all, the Genoese remained at the helm on the island for several centuries. For the same reason, the contemporary autonomist and in-dependence movement cannot be described as power achieved in Weberian terms, because the French government's determination to keep the island within its fold appears today to be as strong as ever. In both the vendetta and the con-temporary eras, the Genoese and French states enjoyed what Weber referred to as the legitimate monopoly over the instruments of force. Institutionalized power may be more appropriately referred to as ideological rather than legiti-mate power, but this does not reduce its impact. With the sophistication of the modern media, and their instrumental connection to the state, the possibility that a rebellious sector of society will control the discourse of a dispute is re-mote. When this fact is combined with the means of economic manipulation and military might available to the state, what seems surprising is that independence aspirations persist over the generations. Could this be interpreted as evidence that motives other than sheer power condition the actions of human beings?

PARADISE

For a couple of reasons, I have left this case study, which compares a village in the heartland of rural Ontario during the 1950s and 1980s (Barrett 1994), to the last. In contrast to the relative uniqueness of the three preceding cases, Paradise (a pseudonym) is a wholly unremarkable little community. Its dramas, to the extent that there have been any, have been small affairs. For most of its existence, which began when settlers made it their home in the last quarter of the nineteenth century, it has drifted contentedly from one decade to the next. In some superficial respects it was similar to Olowo, thus neatly bringing us back to the type of social unit with which we began this chapter. The two villages were almost the same in population size, and Paradise too was run by a powerful elite, but not one that promised anything remotely comparable to everlasting life. As in Olowo, there was a big idea in Paradise, albeit almost unarticulated: the sense of community. And by the 1980s Paradise experienced its own brand of revolutionary change, which transformed it from a sleepy little village to a pulsating commuter town. If ever there was a case to test the hypothesis that the mere mention of power, especially structural power, illuminates those social situations relatively devoid of conflict, Paradise, at least during the 1950s, was it.

We begin by stepping into the chambers of the village council, because back in the 1950s it was there that power was displayed and exercised. Since the village had been founded, the elected members of council had consisted entirely of the leading businessmen and professional people. The head of the council was the reeve, and one man had occupied that position for almost 15 years. He was the wealthiest man in the community, as his father had been before him, and either owned or had a finger in almost every important business. It sometimes was remarked that no new enterprises were established in Paradise because if the reeve didn't own them, he didn't want them. According to elderly residents in the 1980s who retained a vivid memory of the famous reeve, he would either arbitrarily tell prospective entrepreneurs hoping to settle in Paradise to look elsewhere, or keep them waiting so long for a green light that they would get fed up and move on—an apt example of the tactic of the non-decision. During the 1980s, incidentally, I came across another clear case of the non-decision ploy. A newcomer whose business had taken off like a rocket approached one of the service clubs with the intention of becoming a member. Months went by with no response, and eventually he lost interest. The former president of the service organization candidly explained what had transpired. The newcomer was a Jew, and for that reason not welcome. The president simply made sure that the man's application was never processed.

Not only did members of the elite take turns sitting on the council, but there also was a close link between formal and informal power. Notable figures not on the council ran the various service clubs, and took charge of community-wide celebrations and disasters, such as the fall fair and the periodic winter storms that paralyzed the community and occasionally cut it off from the outside world. Only in connection to sports activities, especially hockey and baseball, did people in the classes below the elite assume leadership positions; the exception was the curling club, which was the elite's special baby. The council had the power to control almost everything that happened in the village, such as whether or not a man could put an addition on his house. Savvy individuals wishing to do so would never go directly to the council with a formal request. Instead they would first approach council members informally, as well as influential citizens not on council at the time. Only then did it make sense to place the case before the reeve.

The stratification system in the 1950s was polarized into a small upper class and a large lower class, with an amorphous middle and lower-middle class between them. When asked to describe the class system as it existed then, Paradise people had no difficulty with the extremes; indeed, their usual procedure was to actually name those who belonged to either the upper or lower class; but they were much less certain about who should be placed in the middle sector. To some extent, wealth and power were reflected in residential location. Many of the poorest people lived on two streets bordering the village dump. They had the reputation of being heavy drinkers, and it was also contended that incest among them was rampant. It was on these streets that one found most of the "characters." This was almost an endearing term for men (and some women) who hit the bottle hard. While heavy drinking was just as prevalent among the elite, it was much less visible. The village leaders were inclined to indulge behind closed doors, while lower-class individuals could be found crumpled in an alley. When a wealthy man was discovered inebriated in his car, he was taken home by the courteous local policeman. The "characters" were tossed in jail for the night.

Occasionally there were signs of force being exercised. For example, a rumor spread that a child molester had taken up residence in the village. The reeve paid him a visit and ordered him to pack his bags. The man complied. Generally, however, the basis of power was ideology, the view that the top businessmen and the professionals were the most capable and the most moral citizens, and therefore had both a right and a duty to govern. Since that attitude had prevailed for more than 75 years, it can be said that traditional power, in Weber's sense, operated then in Paradise.

Firming up the ideological basis of power was religion. There were two main denominations in Paradise, the Anglican and United churches. No businessman could afford not to belong to one of them, although membership and attendance were two different things. As long as a person put in an appearance at Christmas and Easter, and was generous with financial contributions, all was well. In one of the churches, the names of those who had made the largest contributions (apart from the weekly collection plate) were posted annually on its bulletin board.

Although resistance supposedly is power's shadow, one would hardly know that from the Paradise case. The elite pretty well had its way, assisted by an ideology that assigned everyone a position along the stratification ladder, with the added wrinkle that nobody's position was expected to change—either upward or downward. This does not mean that people in the lower class were pleased with the situation. Some of them referred to the elite as the establishment, the aristocracy, the hierarchy, the KKK, or simply the Klan. If that constituted resistance, however, it was a rather feeble version. A man who grew up in one of the poorest families in the village, and burned with resentment, explained how he fought back. He would get roaring drunk and boast to "the Klan" that he was a better man than any of them. Then there was the individual, in the 1960s still a relative newcomer to the village, who fought a running battle with the establishment. During each local election he would run for reeve on a platform that the incumbent was a fool and corrupt up to the gills. Although he never received more than a handful of votes, I suppose his actions did constitute a more genuine expression of resistance.

During the decades when the famous reeve ruled the roost, he rarely was opposed at election time. There was one notable exception. A strong-willed man, the owner of a moderately successful business, but definitely not one of the elite, became incensed when the reeve refused to allow him to open a pool hall. This was not because the reeve had an ethical opposition. Rather it was because he owned the building in which the existing pool hall was located. The local election was just around the corner, and the aspiring pool hall owner decided to run for reeve. The election that year was a fiesty affair, but it came to an abrupt end when the incumbent announced his withdrawal, apparently because he was not prepared to have his ethics challenged. His opponent was shocked. He told me that he had never expected to win the election; his purpose was merely to make the perennial reeve dance on a few hot coals. He too withdrew his candidacy, but not before he persuaded a man who was a bona fide member of the elite to replace him. The person who had been reeve for 15 years came back in the late 1950s for one more term in office. But his days in the sunshine, and those of the traditional elite in general, were clearly numbered. In 1959, for the first time in the village's history, an individual who was not one of the elite became reeve. As we shall see next, that was a sign of the far-reaching changes that were to sweep across Paradise in the decades ahead.

In 1951 Paradise had a population of 1,184, virtually unchanged from 1901 when it had been 1,188. By the 1980s the community had almost tripled in size. In what has been referred to as the great population turnaround or reverse migration (Schwarzweller 1979:7), people in urban Ontario began to move to rural areas. While some of them were middle and upper-middle class individuals eager for the tranquility of small-town life, or more preferably the privacy of a country home on 100 acres, the vast majority were working-class families searching for affordable housing.

The impact on the community was dramatic. In the 1950s Paradise had been homogeneous in terms of ethnicity and religion. Fully 99 percent of the residents were Protestants who traced their origins to Northern Ireland. By the 1980s one-fifth of the population was non-British, and included among the newcomers were people from India, Pakistan, and the West Indies, some of them with their roots in Canada dating back several generations. Many of the other newcomers were "white ethnics," a term often used to refer to people from Eastern (and sometimes Southern) Europe. Whereas anti-Catholicism, symbolized by the thriving Orange Order, had been the main basis of prejudice in the 1950s, by the 1980s it had been pushed aside by ethnic and racial consciousness, occasionally leading to physical confrontations. The religious landscape also was transformed. A wide variety of Protestant demoninations made their appearance, including the fundamentalist and evangelical varieties, and not just Catholics but Jews, Buddhists, Muslims, Sikhs, and Hindus settled in Paradise. One consequence was that the close relationship between organized religion and village power disintegrated. A membership in the Anglican or United Church was no longer a prerequisite for business and political success. Indeed, some of the new religious groups wanted nothing to do with mundane matters.

As a result of all these changes, the sense of community began to crumble. Natives of Paradise complained that people no longer "neighbored" like they used to, and some of them, with strangers in their midst, confided that they were frightened to walk the streets—xenophobia in action. Whereas in the past people looked out for each other's children, and generally resolved disputes informally, in the 1980s the local police complained that they were summoned even if a cat strolled into a neighbor's back yard. Paradise increasingly became divided into two communities—the one experienced by the natives, the other by the newcomers. The natives realized that their community had changed forever, but it was still home. As the shock waves generated by the invasion of the reverse migrants subsided, many of the elderly citizens mended the old community bonds during afternoon teas and card games. The newcomers, with the city as their model, never realized that the bonds had been frayed.

There were immense changes to the stratification system. As stated earlier, in the 1950s people readily identified the polar positions of the class system, but struggled with the middle section. In the 1980s exactly the reverse was true. There was a tendency to argue that almost everyone was middle class—native and newcomer alike—and that extreme wealth and poverty no longer existed. It was correct that the middle class was larger and the lower class smaller than in the past. But even more important was that the polar extremes of the class system had ceased to be visible. Wealthy people, as I shall explain in more detail shortly, had stopped running in local elections; and unlike the 1950s, when the poor were to some degree segregated residentially, by the 1980s they were hidden away in rooming houses or in small apartments over the stores.

Power, too, had lost its visibility. In the 1950s the members of the elite, whether or not they were on the council, stood out for everyone to see. In the 1980s, when I asked who had power, many respondents said nobody did. Occasionally a person pointed a finger at the provincial government, implying that it now ran local communities. This was not entirely untrue. To a considerable extent, traditional power had given way to bureaucratic power, sometimes with positive benefits. For example, it was no longer remotely possible that the reeve (or mayor, because Paradise's increased population had converted it from a village to a town) had the power to decide whether or not people would be permitted to add rooms to their houses.

Nowhere were the changes in the community more evident than in the local council. Whereas the elite had previously assumed it was its right and duty to serve on the council, by the 1980s the class level of council members had dropped to the middle and lower-middle, and what drew many of the candidates was the prospect of remuneration. An exception was the 1982 election, when for the first time in two decades a wealthy businessman decided to run for mayor. His victory seemed almost guaranteed, because the incumbent had made a mess of his personal life; his mistress had taken a new lover, and one evening, under the influence of alcohol, he confronted them with a shotgun (fortunately, nobody was harmed). Nevertheless, the incumbent was re-elected. One reason was the sympathy vote. His enemies had broadcast his behavior far and wide (even newspapers in Toronto had picked up the story). People thought he had suffered enough humiliation, and the fact that he was contrite didn't hurt his cause. The other reason was his opponent's wealth and success. He reminded people too much of the famous reeve of the 1950s. As one man put it, his fellow citizens didn't like their leaders to be too clever.

The 1988 election also was noteworthy. For the first time in the community's history, a woman was elected to head the council. Lower-middle class in background, she had known hard times. Her husband was often too ill to hold a job, and she had cleaned houses and taken in laundry to put bread on the table. It was evident that the salary that went with the office of mayor was an incentive to her. The reasons for her successful campaign also were apparent. The former mayor had finally been put in jail. With Paradise people humiliated by his actions, what they wanted more than anything else was a leader not remotely like him. The woman who succeeded him was the obvious choice.

Paradise, let it be clear, was not a case in which the elite had been defeated by the democratic process. Instead, wealthy businessmen and professional people simply withdrew from the political realm, more interested in expanding their business interests beyond Paradise, and more likely to interact with friends who shared their class position in the urban centers to the south. Some businessmen went as far as to claim that a seat on the council was a liability for their businesses. That was because the council no longer had much power, but nevertheless was blamed for the problems pressing the growing population: inadequate sewage disposal, overcrowded schools, and (perceived) increased levels of crime.

If Paradise was examined in the 1950s with the Hunter–Dahl debate on community power in mind, Hunter would have emerged triumphant, because there very definitely was a power elite. By the 1980s, however, the Dahl perspective appeared to have greater plausibility. A seat on the council was within the reach even of lower-middle-class people, and while an economic elite did exist in the town, it did not automatically pull the political strings from behind the public stage. From the perspective of the majority of Paradise residents, power, to the extent that it existed, was dispersed among the various interest groups, rather than the personal resource of the privileged. Yet that frame of mind was partly the result of a discourse that placed everyone in the middle class—one big, egalitarian family. Moreover, it overlooked the degree to which the provincial and federal governments had intruded into the town; in other words, it failed to appreciate the fact that despotic power, whether at the local or societal level, had been replaced by infrastructural power.

One final point: It would appear that the mere mention of power does enhance explanation in situations devoid of major conflict. It reminds us that in the 1950s Paradise was ruled by an entrenched elite despite the emphasis put on shared community values. It also exposes the shallowness of the egalitarian edifice (we're all middle class) in the 1980s. Yet even in a case of relative tranquility such as Paradise, the mere detection of the operation of power is just the analytic starting point. As in the other three case studies presented in this chapter, the stratification system has to be described, ideology unmasked, and manipulation and force documented.

A COMPARISON OF THE FOUR CASES

In each of the three cases dealt with by Wolf, there was a big idea: potlatch among the Kwakiutl, human sacrifice among the Aztecs, and genocide in Hitler's Germany. In the four cases introduced in this chapter, there also was a central idea, with another one hovering in the background. In Olowo it was immortality and then development. Among the racists and anti-Semites in the far right it was the belief in racial superiority and the concern that white people faced extinction. In Corsica it was vengeance and liberty, while Paradise people paid homage to "community" and the related notion that everyone knew his or her place, at least during the 1950s.

Each of the four cases also underwent significant social change: in Olowo from communalism to capitalism, in Corsica from the vendetta era to the contemporary independence era, in Paradise from homogeneity to heterogeneity; it could also be argued that there was a shift in organized racism and anti-Semitism from the sanitary decades of the 1940s and 1950s to the overt neo-Fascism of the 1970s and 1980s, although this arbitrarily cuts history off at World War II.

While there was no single form of power in any of the four cases, there was a dominant combination of forms in each setting, which to some extent was affected by the major changes that occurred. In Olowo, charismatic authority, ideology, and force dominated the early years of the community, force and ideology the later years, with some evidence of manipulation in both eras. Among the racists and anti-Semites, at least following World War II, ideology in the form of propaganda prevailed, and then force (or at least a discourse of force) and manipulation. In Paradise there clearly was a shift from traditional to bureaucratic authority, with power in the 1950s propped up alternatively by ideology and force; by the 1980s there was much less evidence of force, but that did not mean power had dissipated; instead, the impersonal hand of the provincial and federal governments became the puppeteer. The Corsican case was somewhat different in that the same combination of types of power—force, manipulation, and ideology—bridged both the vendetta and contemporary eras.

In all four cases the past was romanticized by a discourse which minimized conflict and power. Olowo people talked about the glory days, when the village was first founded, and harmony and cooperation prevailed, inspired by communalism and the certainty of everlasting life; what they forgot were the frenzied power struggles among the prophets, the members who managed to defect, and the beatings laid on those who were disobedient. Members of the radical right longed for the days when it was respectable to be a racist and anti-Semite, and Canada was a white man's country; overlooked was the vigorous resistance that countered each phase of far right activity. With murder and intimidation associated with the independence movement as their reference point, Corsicans mused about a bygone era when the villages in the mountains were bustling, rather than half-deserted as they are today, when the family unit provided all the pleasures required in life, divorce was virtually unknown, and pollution too; conveniently left out was the raging vendetta, the bandits (not all of them Robin Hoods), and the sheer proverty that prevailed, even among the feudal nobility in its final days. For the natives of Paradise who still lived there in the 1980s, the 1950s were remembered as a period of harmony and belonging, when drugs were unheard of and people knew how to neighbor. But what about "the aristocracy," the alcoholics, and the elderly people at the bottom of the social scale, struggling to survive in an era when social programs such as Medicare must still have seemed a distant dream?

What may be surprising is that in none of the four cases, including unremarkable Paradise, were persuasion and influence much in evidence. The explanation has a lot to do with the arbitrary manner in which I have defined these concepts. In my perspective persuasion is so fundamental to human interaction that it borders on invisibility. Persuasion is intrinsic to communication, almost as basic as language itself. In any social relationship, persuasion seeps back and forth between individuals and traverses the space between them as readily as the air they breathe. Human interaction and persuasion are much the same thing. This largely explains why persuasion was neither evident in nor the focus of the case studies. Its universality robs it of an analytic cutting edge. Moreover, as soon as one person attempts to persuade another person to do something—that is, as soon as persuasion becomes conscious and deliberate—it begins to be transformed into one of the other forms of power such as force, manipulation, or authority. Recall the famous mafia line: "I made him an offer he couldn't refuse." On the surface this reads like persuasion, but the subtext suggests coercion.

Influence in my lexicon is a more general term than persuasion. Indeed, influence rather than power could plausibly be treated as the master concept, with authority and force at its polar reaches, and manipulation off on another tangent. My definition of influence is essentially the same as Bailey's definition (1980) of persuasion. While definitions are undoubtedly arbitrary, presumably the person doing the defining thinks that they have analytic utility. In my case, I prefer power as the master concept because more so than influence it highlights what I assume to be the explanatory core of human interaction: force, manipulation, and ideologically conditioned authority. Of course, this concentrates the investigation of power at one end of the scale, where conflict, ideology, and stratification are located, whereas influence (or persuasion in Bailey's approach) occupies a position in the middle, and for that reason might be regarded as more neutral and objective. Yet as Weber (1949:10) wisely observed, the middle position along a continuum is no more value-free than either extreme.

Given my focus on what have been termed the negative sanctions associated with power, it is possible that I have under-represented what several other writers have stressed: the positive aspects of power. Certainly the spectacular economic success of Olowo was partly a result of the *oba*'s immense power. As for Paradise, one man who had sat on council during the 1950s said he didn't like the famous reeve very much, but he did respect him, because with the minimum of fuss (and opposition) he got things done and kept the village perking along. However, power appears, especially in the long run, to have been more positive for some people than for others. In the West African utopia, it was the third *oba* and his cronies who emerged from the shift to capitalism smelling of roses; and for almost a century in Paradise, harmony and stability translated into the sustained privilege of the upper class. Without the production of power, the price paid by society might be apathy, anomy, and even atrophy. Yet while power may render human accomplishments possible, it would be naive to think that everyone benefits to the same degree, or that individual potential and achievement always coincide.

In closing, I want to return to the debate over agency (voluntaristic, deliberate) and structural (institutional, unintentional) power, and the related issue of not-power. There is something intuitively attractive about Weber's perspective: power is the capacity, despite resistance, to impose one's will on another. Yet in every case that I can think of which conforms to Weber's approach, power is backed up by social structural conditions and related ideologies. For example, the first *oba* in Olowo had the power to force competitors from the community, and punish deviants severely. But his power was sanctioned by religious beliefs that dominated every aspect of village life, and enhanced by the communal system which allowed him to direct and control his subjects, as well as by the authority inherent in the title of *oba*. The implication is that power is more meaningfully conceived in social structural terms. Yet it is just as plausible to argue that behind what looks like the impersonal impact of social structure lie active human agents—individuals deliberately making decisions and influencing and manipulating others. In other words, we are back on the merry-go-round. How to get off it? The obvious solution, and the one which I prefer, is to combine agency and structure in a single conceptual scheme. Of course, that is somewhat akin to announcing that one supports motherhood. Yet it does help us avoid a dead-end theoretical direction in the literature on power. I am thinking of Wrong's recommendation that power be restricted to agency so that not everything in society is power. That approach, in my judgment, is a dead-end because it arbitrarily strips power from social structure, the weight and shape of which are patently significant for the fates of individual actors.

My suggestion is that we avoid treating power as a constant across the scope of human interaction and society in a different way: we distinguish between power, which embraces both agency and structure; and not-power, which also means not-conflict, not-ideology, and not-stratification, and embraces harmony and cooperation. The obvious objection is that this merely lands us back on a different merry-go-round: the eternal conflict–consensus controversy. Yet if we want to understand both the big and small issues of human interaction, from multinational corporations to family dynamics around the dinner table, we have to examine both structure and agency, and assign as much causal weight to conflict as to consensus. Besides, the notion that we have to choose between the conflict and consensus models is misleading. Conflict and consensus are dialectically entwined. Not only do they have a mutual impact, but sometimes they fade into each other, changing their appearances, and thus obfuscating social interaction. In the context of this study, there possibly is no more apt example than culture itself. In decades past, culture looked like the epitome of consensus and harmony; yet arguably underneath it hierarchy and conflict flourished.

PEEKING INTO THE FUTURE

Intellectual fads come and go. Culture, once the shining concept in the American school, can hardly be labelled a fad, but it certainly has lost its luster in recent years. Power, hitherto a neglected term in the discipline, has been dusted off and placed on display. Yet its lifespan remains uncertain. Will it, and culture too, blossom or wither in this new millennium? Forecasting the future is a treacherous business, a game more often lost than won, but here goes. My prediction is that the culture concept will endure into the decades ahead, and may even capture some of its past glory, while the power concept will slip back to the periphery where it previously gathered moss, its brief day in the sunshine a footnote in academic history.

There are several reasons for painting culture's future in bright colors. One is that even if the trend toward global cultural similarity continues, it is improbable that total uniformity will be attained, or that local culture will be entirely eclipsed or fail to develop new forms. In other words, culture will remain a variable to be reckoned with in anthropological investigation.

Another reason is that there are too many parties with a vested interest in holding onto culture to allow it to slide into oblivion. Recall the backlash against the critique of culture mounted by scholars such as Lewis. For many field workers and applied anthropologists the raging debate about the concept must have come across as a monumental bore. From their perspective, culture, unexamined and unchallenged, gives them what they want: a label to put on their activity, thus locating it in academic space and distinguishing it from other disciplines. Counter-disciplines such as culture studies, ethnic studies, and multicultural studies demand considerably more from culture. When joined to power, it becomes the critical variable in explaining which groups get the biggest slice of the pie. Without culture, field workers and applied researchers could always fall back on social structure, but the counter-disciplines would lack a rationale to exist.

It should also be pointed out that at the very moment when culture has been attacked from within—that is, by anthropologists themselves—it has finally caught on in other disciplines. There now are subdisciplines of cultural geography, cultural sociology, and cultural psychology. The scholars in these subdisciplines will find it curious indeed if we inform them that for the past 100 years or so we have got it all wrong about culture. Then there is the lay person's perspective. The proverbial man or woman on the street, having only recently discovered culture, will not be quick to give it up. For lay people, culture is a user-friendly concept. It connotes ethnicity rather than race, invites the celebration of diversity, and encourages people to take pride in their tolerance. Its very vagueness assures that it won't mutate into political consciousness or challenge the status quo.

If culture is a cuddly concept, power is a prickly one. It unsettles the mind. It reminds people of the gap between rich and poor, and makes them skeptical of authority. Ordinary people are not disinterested in power. To the contrary, they are acutely aware that success and failure in life depend as much on who you know and what you can get away with as on individual drive and capacity. This brings us to the main reason why power's new-found celebrity will eventually fade. From the perspective of the state, big business, and the privileged in general, unobfuscated power is dangerous power. The challenge is to render power as vague, and therefore as innocuous, as culture. Enter ideology, discourse, and manipulation. Little wonder that the lay person's interest in power dissipates, and incipient resistance falls flat.

In mounting this argument, I do not want to suggest that power will cease to be an important issue in the academic world. In fact, if my interpretation is valid that a new problematic has emerged in anthropology, one that problematizes difference and profiles stratification, the focus on power will be reinforced. However, social science doesn't enjoy great prestige in the outside world, and is unlikely to have much impact on state policy or big business. Besides, academics are citizens too, vulnerable to the same ideological forces that shape the consciousness of lay people. Witness, for example, the alacrity by which some academics, with dollar signs in their eyes, have bought into the notion that the aims of the university and the business world should harmonize.

What all this suggests is that it will require a lot more effort to make sure that power is still a key concept in the decades ahead than culture. When culture met power in the 1980s and 1990s, culture was the first to blink. But in the long run it may be culture that has the last laugh.[3]

NOTES

1. A fifth phase materialized in the late 1980s and 1990s, when the far right began to use the Internet to promote its views and recruit members, but that came after my research had been finished. For information and analysis on the Internet and the far right, see Hier (2000).

2. These initials stand for the following: ARC (L'Action Régionaliste Corse), FLNC (Le Front de Libération Nationale de la Corse), MPA (Mouvement pour l'Autodétermination), FRANCIA (Front d'Action Nouvelle Contre l'Indépendence et l'Autonomie).

3. If a note of regret was detected in these last sentences, that was my intention, and the reasons are twofold. First, power may not be a magic bullet, but we are better armed intellectually with it than without it. Second, in my judgment it is unfortunate that culture and power ever were opposed in the first place. It is much more profitable, as Wolf argues, to view them as intrinsically interconnected.

Postscript: Culture Meets Power at the World Trade Center and the Pentagon

This may well be a good time to be an anthropologist, but in view of the terrorist attack on America—a poignant reminder that the mixture of power and culture sometimes produces tragedy on a grand scale—it is not such a good time to be a human being. September 11, 2001, with four hijacked commercial jet liners transformed into explosive missiles, joins Pearl Harbor and the assassination of President Kennedy as defining moments in Western consciousness—perhaps even global consciousness. The intentional crashing of the passenger airplane into the Pentagon, and the horrific destruction of another one in Pennsylvania, possibly after passengers had grappled with their assailants, would have been enough to stamp that day into our brains. But earlier there was the World Trade Center. With people around the globe glued to their television sets, stunned by the image of the north tower smoking and crumbling after being struck by an airplane, the absolute incredible occurred: before our eyes, yet another jet liner loomed onto the television screens, silent and menacing, and with deadly accurate aim plowed into and pulverized the south tower.

Years ago, when studying organized racism and anti-Semitism in Canada, I came to realize that some events and situations are so traumatic that scholarly analysis, at least in the short run, is an unaffordable luxury; what is needed first is support, compassion and action.[1] September 11 is such a situation. Nevertheless I have decided to comment on it because it goes to the heart of this book—the relationship between culture and power. Let me make it clear that I shall only be considering the events of September 11 in terms of the arguments mounted in previous chapters. To attempt more than this, especially since I am putting these thoughts down on paper less than three weeks after the terrorist attack, when it is far from clear what the response of America and its allies will be and just how much the world will change, would be unforgivably foolish. My modest hope is that the preceding analysis of culture and power will throw some light on the essential (but perhaps unwelcome) question regarding September 11: why?

1. EMOTIONAL AND COMMUNITY RESPONSE

For Americans, this was not a natural disaster such as an earthquake, or a catastrophe that occurred in some distant land, the scale of which is often difficult to appreciate despite media coverage. Instead, it was an intentional attack carried out on American soil, and it probably was deliberately planned in a manner that would exploit its maximum impact—the eye-witness accounts of millions of television viewers in the United States and around the globe as the second tower of the World Trade Center was destroyed.

In the hours that followed the attack, stunned disbelief and trauma gave way to other emotions and bewildering questions. How could human beings do something so evil? Why do they hate Americans so much? Soon both defiance and resilience began to emerge alongside grief. Cries to "nuke the bastards," whoever they were, echoed next to calls to close ranks and get the nation back on its feet. Red Cross drop-off centers for goods and financial contributions sprang up, and citizens lined up to donate blood. The terrorist attack, of course, was as symbolic as it was physical. The World Trade Center represented the core of capitalism, the Pentagon the nation's military might, and it may well be that the target of the hijacked jet liner that crashed in Pennsylvania was the political heart of America, the White House. The reaction of Americans was equally symbolic. Candles flickered everywhere, and American flags dominated the landscape. They hung from car windows and from the purses and clothing of pedestrians. The upsurge of patriotism was palpable—and this in a nation that people in other countries sometimes thought had already been excessive. When members of Congress broke out into an apparently spontaneous singing of "God Bless America," it appeared that the nation had symbolically become a single community.

2. ECONOMIC AND POLITICAL RESPONSE

With the odor of a recession already in the air, the last thing that the American economy needed was a kick in the gut, but that's what it got. The New York Stock Exchange was shut down and the nation's business was put on hold. Airports were closed, and all commercial traffic grounded, with dozens of planes diverted to Canada. The land border between the United States and Canada became clogged with truck traffic, due to beefed-up inspections. Realizing that the probable intention of the terrorists to cripple the world's strongest economy was working all too well, President Bush and New York's mayor Rudolph Giuliani urged Americans to get back to normal—show up at the office, go to restaurants, and spend money. One week after the terrorist attack (Monday, September 17), the New York Stock Exchange had a rocky reopening, but what was important was that it was once again functioning. Airports were declared safe for business, with promises of new security measures, such as more vigilant passenger inspection and possibly sky marshals and fortified cockpits. Nevertheless, air traffic was sharply reduced, as people cancelled holidays, their apprehensions not calmed by the government's decision to shoot down any hijacked craft that threatened targets on the ground.

In a display of bipartisan unity, Congress made $40 billion available for rebuilding New York and the Pentagon, and for erecting defenses against attack and chasing down the terrorists. The spotlight was turned on one individual, Osama bin Laden. Born into a wealthy family in Saudi Arabia in 1957, and a follower of the Wahhabi sect of Sunni Muslims, bin Laden had for years been on America's most wanted list. He allegedly had been involved at least indirectly in the 1993 bombing of the World Trade Center, and it was believed that he had helped finance and train people for other terrorist projects such as the bombing of American embassies in Tanzania and Kenya. In 1994 Saudi Arabia revoked his citizenship and his family disowned him. In 1996, as a result of American diplomatic pressure, he was forced to leave Sudan. He quickly resurfaced in Afghanistan, where ironically he had earlier been supported by the Americans who had aided with Afghanistan in its decade-long war in the 1980s against the former Soviet Union.

The Taliban government in Afghanistan, recognized only by Pakistan, Saudi Arabia and the United Arab Emirates, was the first to feel the heat of America's anger. President Bush ordered the Taliban to hand over bin Laden and close down the terrorist training camps within its borders. While the American government declared that its demands were non-negotiable, and that failure to comply would be harshly dealt with, it is improbable that it seriously thought the Taliban would cooperate. And in fact it did not, making its own demand for hard, incontrovertible evidence that bin Laden was guilty.

The American government then turned its attention to Pakistan, an impoverished nation with a military government and a nuclear capacity that shares its border with Afghanistan. In an unusual display of brute power, the Americans presented Pakistan with a choice: either cooperate by closing its border with Afghanistan, shutting off supplies to bin Laden, sharing intelligence information about his movements, and making available air and ground space for the American military, or risk annihilation as a country. Despite widespread anti-American sentiments and militant fundamentalists within Pakistan, and the realization that lining up on America's side would be tantamount to waging war not only on a neighbor but also on a fellow-Muslim state, President Musharraf of Pakistan did just that. Presumably he had concluded that there was no other option, at least if his country was to survive and if he was still going to be its leader.

Globalization notwithstanding, domestic issues and a mildly isolationist foreign policy had marked the presidency of Clinton (the Middle East conflict being the main exception), a trend that became more pronounced after Bush assumed office. One of the most significant and immediate consequences of the attack on America is that its isolationist stance evaporated, at least for the moment. The American government began to build an international coalition to combat terrorism, arguing cogently that terrorism is everybody's problem, not just America's. Out of these efforts emerged a potentially profound shift in global alliances. Of course, countries like Britain and Canada were on its side from the beginning, and as time went on Britain's Prime Minister, Tony Blair, emerged as a leading player in the war against terrorism. Western European leaders, previously somewhat unimpressed by Bush, expressed their solidarity with America, and in France the newspaper *Le Monde*, often critical of the United States, proclaimed: "We are all Americans."

So horrific was the terrorist attack that expressions of sympathy poured in even from America's rivals and enemies—countries such as Iran, Libya, Sudan, China, and Russia. No doubt the motivations varied from one country to the next. Virtually all Muslim nations include factions of militant fundamentalists, and care had to be taken not to be too effusive in sympathy toward America. China and Russia, also faced with rebellious Muslims within their borders, had much less to lose. By sending its condolences to the United States, China may have calculated that its civil rights record no longer would be as great a barrier to its international trading ambitions. As for Russia, given the possibility that bin Laden operatives were active in Chechnya, greater understanding for its efforts to control the rebels was anticipated from the American government. But this was only the tip of Russian expectations. By allowing the American military to operate from bases in Russia's satellite countries bordering on Afghanistan, President Putin may have hoped that Russia's acceptance into the Western Hemisphere would be enhanced, paving the way for eventual membership in NATO.

Iran's sympathy was perhaps the most surprising of all. But the Iranians had no love for the Taliban, partly because Iranians are Shiite Muslims and Afghans are Sunni Muslims. Besides, Prime Minister Tony Blair's earlier overtures to Iran had already paved the way for a thaw between that country and America. Less surprising was America's renewed interest in Indonesia. As the largest Muslim state in the world, with its own share of militant fundamentalists, Indonesia suddenly took an exceptional importance for American foreign policy.

As America settled down to mourn its dead and clean up the disasters in New York, Washington and Pennsylvania, and with the coalition against terrorism rounding into shape, it was clear that a lot of things had changed. Despite an apparent shaky beginning, President Bush eventually found his voice, and the question marks around the legitimacy of his presidency faded. His approval rating soared dramatically, as had his father's earlier in the war with Iraq. Star Wars appeared to be more and more irrelevant in a world that demanded hand-to-hand combat and an efficient infrastructure of firefighters, medical personnel, and intelligence experts. Even the hard line against big government seemed to temporarily soften as people looked to the nation's leaders for answers and solutions.

3. DECLARATION OF WAR

Less than a week after the events of September 11, President Bush proclaimed war on terrorism, labeling it the first war of the twenty-first century. From the outset, there was clear recognition that this would not be a conventional war, nor would it be quickly won. Terrorism is too amorphous to expect anything else. While it may be supported by individual states, its organizational structure, to the extent that there is one, may stretch across several states, with loose unions between various groups, much the same as obtained for the far right organizations that I studied in Canada. Moreover, given the cell structure of such organizations, the individuals who actually perform the acts of terror may never have met people higher up in the command structure. A case in point is Osama bin Laden's organization, al Qaeda (Arabic for *the base*).

Who are these terrorists? Contrary to public opinion, they are not necessarily individuals who have known nothing but poverty. According to Robbins (1999:349), the typical militant is young, college-educated, and unemployed, and embraces fundamentalist Islam as an alternative to Westernization. This profile accords with Nash's findings (1991) in Malaysia, and it is remarkably similar to the profile of radical right members in North America (many of them Christian fundamentalists), including those I examined in Canada. As Lipset and Raab observed (1970), the far right in America constitutes "extremism of the center."

What motivates them? While this question will be addressed more fully below, suffice it to say that enormous religious fervor encapsulating the sentiments of implacable injustice, spirited nationalism, and the politics of identity is a large part of the answer, even if it rests on a bedrock of global political and economic patterns traced back to the advent of colonialism and capitalism. Without such fervor, it would be difficult to explain the willingness of an individual to sacrifice his own life to serve a cause, and perhaps even more incomprehensible how he could coldly and brutally murder thousands of innocent civilians.[2]

How could less than two dozen terrorists have such enormous impact on the world? The simple answer is that it often does not require an army to change the course of history, or at least to get the world's attention. It used to be said that in some Third World countries it only required a dozen committed junior army officers with rifles to carry out a *coup d'état*. Similarly, back in the 1960s in Canada, a single member of the far right, David Stanley, travelled by bus halfway across the country, dropping racist literature wherever it stopped. A traumatized nation feared that the forces of fascism were on the move.

Why is terrorism regarded as evil incarnate? One reason is that it is often (but not always) an attack on civilians, and the perpetrators are individuals consumed by feelings of injustice and hatred, rather than states competing for straightforward advantage. Another reason is that like a boxer who continues to pummel his opponent after the latter is out on his feet, or a maniac who repeatedly stabs his victim long after life has stopped, there is a gratuitous element to terrorism—a desire not just to destroy, but to do it in the most hideous manner possible. Having said this, it must be added that gratuitous violence also has a rational component, at least from the terrorist's perspective; that is because the intended victims are not just the people who are maimed or killed—but everyone connected to them. A third reason is that unlike conventional warfare, where rules apply, making it possible to identify war criminals, terrorists don't recognize normal rules. This explains why no distinction is made between military and civilian targets, and why the ends justify the means—possibly any means, such as crashing loaded passenger jet liners into civilian targets.

Whereas in times past military service used to be considered an honorable profession, hence the term gentleman soldier, the terrorists who acted on September 11 have been labelled barbarians and cowards. Yet one person's terrorist is often another person's freedom fighter, and it is difficult to avoid the conclusion that just as the definition of a war criminal is to some degree the prerogative of the victor, the same holds for terrorism, although this raises complex questions about relativism. If cowardice is meant to describe the covert and sneaky way in which terrorists operate—never stepping out into the open and fighting the good fight like a man—it too seems inappropriate when applied to terrorists. Terrorism, like guerrilla warfare, exists because the enemy is simply too powerful for direct confrontation. It is possibly the only method that has any hope of success. Malinowski (1941:523) defined war "as an armed contest between two independent political units, by means of organized military force, in the pursuit of tribal or national policy." Because terrorists do not constitute a tribal or state organization, it may be concluded that terrorism is not the equivalent of war. Yet if terrorists are not engaged in war, there can be no war on terrorism.

Semantics aside, there is no doubt that at this point in history terrorism has been defined as beyond the limits of acceptable human action. Just as fascists, racists, and anti-Semites laid low in what have been labelled "the sanitary decades" immediately following World War II, no terrorist (and no state soft on terrorism) would dare to raise his head today. In a sense we have returned to the era of the Cold War, when Western democracies had a simple formula for sorting out good nations from bad: they were either for the West or against it. Any other consideration such as the degree of democracy and free speech was secondary.

4. CRACKS IN THE SOLIDARITY

The United Nations General Assembly voted 189–0 to condemn the terrorist attack on America (Iraq did not vote, apparently because its membership dues were not paid up). This does not mean that people everywhere were grieving. Stories circulated in the media about young Palestinians dancing in the streets, and there was no shortage of foreign commentators who publicly expressed sympathy for the victims but declared that America had got what it deserved—full payment for its alleged economic rape and bully tactics around the globe. Within America there were similar cracks in the nation's solidarity. Looters in New York made the rounds, albeit quickly brought under control by the police and the army. Then, of course, there were the usual despicable characters who attempted to profit from the tragedy by establishing phony philanthropies to which donations for the victims could be sent. Despite the closing of the ranks among the American people and the thirst for revenge, a nascent peace movement soon appeared, its participants drawn partly from the anti-globalization movement. Yet probably the gravest problem of all concerned racism. Arabs, Muslims, and in fact anyone who fit the stereotype of the Middle Easterner, came under attack. Individuals were beaten up and mosques were set on fire.[3]

To the credit of American political leaders, a major effort was made to snuff out these signs of racism. President Bush met publicly with American Muslim leaders. In his September 20 televised speech to the nation, he stated that America respects the Muslim faith, and declared that the terrorists were not true Muslims; they were enemies to their faith. The same message was delivered by some Muslim clerics (*The New York Times*, Sunday, September 20, CY9), who asserted that the fight against terrorism, not terrorism itself, is a holy war.

Even if it is assumed that Bush's concern about racism was genuine, his motivations no doubt were more complex. Perhaps he hoped to avoid the mistakes of the past, such as the internment of Japanese Americans during World War II, or the quick but fallacious assumption that Arab and Muslim fanatics had been responsible for the Oklahoma bombing. Yet there were more pragmatic considerations. With one billion of the faithful, Islam stands second only to Christianity in sheer numbers. What may not be widely appreciated is that seven million of these Muslims live in the United States. Moreover, 20,000 Afghans reside in the Queens district of New York City. While a militant brand of Islam long ago caught on among African Americans, the majority of Muslim immigrants since the 1960s are more conservative (*Time*, September 24, p. 37); in fact, apparently more than 65 percent of them voted for Bush in the last election.

Domestic politics alone, then, might account for Bush's quick steps to confront racist outbreaks, but the international arena was even more critical. With the Middle Eastern origin of the terrorists apparently established—they held passports from Saudi Arabia, the United Arab Emirates, and Lebanon—and with bin Laden as the potential kingpin, and the always volatile Israeli-Palestinian conflict and resentment toward American support of Israel, the last thing the Bush administration needed was another reason for driving Muslims in the Middle East and elsewhere further into the terrorist embrace. This is why Israeli Prime Minister Sharon, who had wrongly misread the attack on America as a green light to go after the Palestinians, was initially rebuked. The worry was that the battle would escalate into a war between Muslim and Arab nations and the West, and even become conceptualized as a clash of civilizations. This may explain why the Bush administration (with suspicious convenience) announced that just before the terrorist attack it had made a decision to promote an independent Palestinian state. The same motivation accounts for the aghast reaction to Italian Prime Minister Silvio Berlusconi's declaration that Western civilization is superior to Islamic civilization, and the pressure on him to withdraw the statement (*Globe and Mail*, Saturday, Sept. 28, A7). Yet in his September 20 address to the nation, Bush himself had stated: "The civilized world is rallying to America's side." In all probability he meant to include nations everywhere sickened by and opposed to terrorism, but that may not have been the way Arabs and Muslims interpreted his comment.

Another victim of the terrorist attack was America's enviable civil rights record. At the same time that President Bush pleaded for tolerance towards Muslims, tolerance for dissent crumpled in a heap. Questions about why terrorism existed, and whether America's actions of the past had in any way inflamed it, were ruled out of order. In a speech to the United Nations on October 1 (*The New York Times*, Tuesday, Oct. 2, B5), Mayor Rudolph Giuliani probably caught the mood of the nation: "Let those who say that we must understand the reasons for terrorism come with me to the thousands of funerals we're having in New York City." Not everyone toed the line, but they paid a price. Susan Sontag, in an article in *The New Yorker*, heaped scorn on government officials and members of the media for parroting the same superficial and obfuscating rhetoric regarding the terrorist attack, and she even had the audacity to suggest that the real cowards are those who drop bombs from 20,000 feet in the sky. Shortly after, Bill Maher, host of the TV show "Politically Incorrect," repeated some of Sontag's charges. Both were severely criticized, with some sponsors withdrawing from Maher's show. Then there was the chilling reaction of Ari Fleischer, President Bush's press secretary. People, he intoned, would be well advised to watch what they said and did.[4]

Although the quote above from Mayor Giuliani's speech almost suggests that any effort to understand the terrorist attack is illegitimate, the fact is that President Bush himself offered his own explanation in his address to the nation on September 20. The terrorists, he stated, hated America for its democracy, its freedom of religion and freedom of speech. Freedom itself, he declared, is under attack. The clear message was that nothing more needed to be said. It is because this explanation is so shallow that it is necessary now to turn to more complex issues and deeper explanations, beginning with the possibility that the Bush administration's policies themselves contributed to the terrorist attack.

Despite the controversial manner in which George W. Bush ended up in the White House, he confidently moved to put his own stamp on America, a mixture of isolationism and big power arrogance that caused even some of America's friends to squirm. Bush dropped out of several international accords such as those intended to ban germ warfare and control global warming, and he announced his determination of going ahead with Star Wars regardless of opposition and concerns among other heads of state that the impact would be to unleash a new phase of nuclear arms competition.

Perhaps in reaction to Clinton's failure to forge peace in the Middle East, Bush opted for a hands-off position unless there was a realistic chance for success. But he did something more. He passed judgment on the battle between the Israelis and the Palestinians, stating clearly that he held the Palestinians responsible for the latest outburst of violence. Then in the fall of 2001 the United States withdrew from the U.N. conference on racism in Durban, South Africa, as a protest against the charges that Israel is a racist state and Zionism a racist movement.[5] If Muslim and Arab leaders did not interpret this withdrawal as further evidence that the United States had taken sides, that would be surprising.[6] However, neither the Bush administration's stance in the Middle East conflict nor its unilateral withdrawal from international accords explains the terrorist attack of September 11, because there is every reason to think that the attack was organized and set in motion long before Bush assumed office. Besides, while America's political agenda under the Bush administration may have been stretched in one direction, this was not to the extent that it had mutated into something never seen before; it remained recognizable as and consistent with American policy since the U.S.A. had become a superpower following the Second World War. Therefore, if the current Bush administration's political agenda fed international terrorism, so too did the agendas of previous administrations. And there is one other point worth making: the disapproval (most of it mild) expressed by the leaders of some Western nations regarding the direction steered by the Bush administration can be dismissed as so much hypocrisy. These leaders have unanimously remained on side in America's war on terrorism, and they will continue to be there long after the rest of the world has lost interest in the events of September 11. This is because American hegemony remains the best guarantee that the power and privilege enjoyed by the industrialized West remain intact despite the ambitions of rival centers of culture and power.

5. GLOBALIZATION

Globalization has not only fragmented local culture and imposed a semblance of universal culture, but it has also contributed to the reversal of a long-standing trend which confounded Marx's prediction that capitalism's internal contradictions would blow it apart. That trend was the emergence of social reforms such as minimal wage legislation, unemployment insurance, medicare, welfare payments, and the hard-won acceptance of trade unions as a positive contribution to capitalist society. As a result of globalization not only have these reforms been cut back in order to enhance economic competitiveness, but in addition the gap between rich and poor nations, and between rich and poor people within nations, has grown broader. In this context, two e-mails which recently appeared on my computer screen are highly relevant. One was a song entitled "Bomb Them with Butter" composed in the wake of the events of September 11 (Gordon 2001). The songwriter's point was that if people in Afghanistan, Pakistan and other countries did not live in squalor, they would be more benevolently disposed towards the West. The same message was made more prosaically in the other e-mail. The suggestion was that if the $40 billion earmarked for the war on terrorism was distributed instead among the people of Afghanistan and other poor countries, terrorism would wither on the vine.[7]

It could be argued, of course, that globalization has actually brought prosperity to the world, and that if tradition in the process has been undermined and stratification broadened, those are acceptable costs. It might even be asserted that holding America responsible for the woes of the world is a classic example of blaming the victim. As the foremost exponent and benefactor of globalization, America is merely the most visible target. Certainly there is a huge leap from resentment, no matter how strongly felt and justified, to the terrorist acts of September 11. Besides, it cannot be argued that one nation—America—dumped globalization onto our laps while simultaneously asserting that globalization is not constrained by the modern state; that indeed it has rendered the state somewhat obsolete. Globalization, it might be observed, is merely an economic program with strong political undertones that has been attempting to shake loose of its parochial and traditional harness since the era of the Enlightenment. Why blame America for its successful emancipation? In this contrast, it is important to appreciate that social change has always generated resentment and protest. In fact, Rose (1971) argued that anti-Semitism has its roots in the association of Jews with the erosion of placid rural society and the emergence of discordant urban life. Lipset and Raab (1970) pointed out that the underlying target of fascists and racists in America was not blacks and Jews but social change itself.

The "blame the victim" syndrome took several other forms following the events of September 11. It was pointed out that America's own record regarding terrorism is not unblemished, Allende's fate in Chile being a prime example. Then, too, some American commentators faulted the American government, especially the intelligence community, for relaxing its guard against terrorism. Somewhat different was the accusation of Jerry Falwell and Pat Robertson, two prominent evangelists, that America deserved the terrorist attack. It was God's retribution for sinful behavior: secularism, loss of faith, banning prayers in schools, and catering to feminists, homosexuals, and civil rights groups (*Globe and Mail*, September 15, 2001, A2).

Finally, it should be made clear that standing alongside resentment toward America is the opposite emotion: admiration. Vidich and Bensman (1958) found that residents of "small-town U.S.A." held contradictory attitudes about big cities: disgust for the chaos and loose values, but admiration for the energy, novelty and individual freedom. Much the same could be said about the attitudes of people around the globe toward America. In the same breath that the United

States is condemned for its treatment of people of color or its pistol-packing culture, thoughts turn to bluejeans, John Wayne, and the fabled American Dream.

6. POWER AND CULTURE

As it has been repeated throughout this study, conflict and power are twins. Whenever situations of large-scale conflict arise, power is front and center. The reverse, of course, is also true: dramatic displays of power are manifestations of underlying conflict. Therefore, what should be least surprising is that the brute power exhibited in the events of September 11 is connected to struggles with deep roots. The big question is whether these struggles are primarily cultural, politico-economic, or some combination of the two. Before addressing this question, a couple of observations about the literature on power are appropriate. First, the argument mounted by Parsons and others that power is always positive looks pretty ridiculous in the context of September 11. Second, the assertion by Parsons, Arendt, and Foucault that force or coercion has nothing to do with power, or by Dahl and Etzioni that force is only one of several components of power, rather than the most fundamental component, looks more dubious by the moment.

In an analysis of "the Troubles" in Northern Ireland, Ruane and Todd (1991) distinguish between cultural explanations (irrational hatred fueled by age-old tradition and religious fanaticism) and structural explanations (inequality and power imbalances institutionalized into the relationships between England, the Irish Republic, and the Unionist and Republican factions in Northern Ireland). In their judgment, cultural explanations are merely the surface manifestation of underlying structural conditions. Whether we employ the term culture or the more politically and morally loaded concept "civilization,"[8] the same might be said about the clash between Muslim and Arab societies and the West: culture (or civilization) is only the shadow on the wall of the cave. Certainly there is considerable evidence that straightforward political struggles and vested economic interests underwrote the September 11 terrorist attack. For example, in recent and current history there is the Palestinian *intifada* (uprising), the American-led war on Iraq and the continuing economic embargo, plus the presence of the American military on the holy land of Saudi Arabia, with the prize of oil visible in the background. Yet there is just as much evidence that cultural and religious factors were motivating forces. For example, from the perspective of militant Muslims, and perhaps even of more moderate individuals, America is the Great Satan: godless, licentious, and materialistic. From the perspective of many Westerners, Muslims are inclined to fanaticism, violence, intolerance, and backwardness. In short, each side demonizes the other, and if demonization is anything it is a form of manipulation.

Like most stereotypes, the above ones bear little relation to reality. Attempts to modernize Islamic nations certainly were evident in Ataturk's Turkey (now the only Muslim state in NATO), and the variation across Muslim and Arab nations, and among people within these countries, is no doubt so immense as to render any generalization, benign or misanthropic, suspect. As for America, what is remarkable for a highly industrialized nation is its religiosity. Ammerman (1991) has indicated that 72 percent of Americans believe the Bible is the word of God, and 39 percent believe the Bible is literally true. And like many Arab and Muslim countries, the United States has its share of fundamentalists—Christian fundamentalists—who exercise a major influence on the country's politics, and whose members have occasionally been moved to extreme violence, such as murdering medical practitioners who perform abortions.

The implication is that it is the interaction of cultural and structural conditions that shapes the course of history. That was essentially Marx's perspective (as emphasized by Engels), despite his insistence that in the long run economics rather than aspects of the superstructure (values, beliefs, ideology) is the prime mover of society. For example, he argued (Selsam et al. 1970:229) that during the Middle Ages opposition to feudalism was manifested not only in armed insurrection but also in mysticism. Similarly, Murphy (1971:218) has observed that while values may be incongruent with interests (or culture with social organization), they are never irrelevant to interests. Even a cursory glance at Muslim history, notably the decline of the Ottoman Empire by the beginning of the nineteenth century, confirms the rich mixture of cultural and structural forces animated by power. As Robbins (1999:348) has indicated, fundamentalist Muslims trace the erosion of Islamic influence and respect on the world scene and the accompanying poverty to a decline in religious faith, which in turn they believe was brought about by Western colonialism and the negative influence of Western culture. Muslim fundamentalism is seen as a vehicle to revive faith in Allah and reassert the superiority of Muslim civilization. What all this suggests in the present world is that if ever there were a clear case to cast doubt on the wisdom of separating and opposing culture and power, and instead to reinforce their interconnectedness, the terrorist attack on America is it. Yet it would be naïve to expect widespread acknowledgment of the overlap between culture and power. Just as the notion of an orderly universe seems to be a necessary fiction that we tell each other, so too is the belief that human beings are graced by the purity of culture, uncontaminated by vested interests and institutionalized inequality.

7. RESISTANCE

In previous chapters it was shown that resistance has been criticized for being romanticized, and for having little impact on society. If the events of September 11 can be labelled an expression of resistance, and I can't see how it could be otherwise interpreted, they surely demonstrate that resistance can be astoundingly effective, rather than mere window dressing.

One of the big questions is whether the hatred buttressed by religious fervor among the terrorists is to some degree dormant in the Muslim and Arab world in general, and whether under certain conditions it might be aroused. There is an even more bothersome question: to what extent does the terrorist attack represent the resistance of losers everywhere to globalization and Western hegemony? Is there a small piece of bin Laden in everyone left behind by globalization?[9] Remember my reference to commentators who asserted that America had gotten what it deserved because of its heavyhanded interference abroad. In this context, it would be surprising if some African Americans did not have mixed feelings about the events of September 11, including doubts about whether the impending battle against the terrorists is their war. From the massive television coverage of the terrorist attack in the weeks that followed it, the viewer would hardly know that African Americans even exist. Perhaps their relative invisibility tells a story.

8. RELATIVISM

I have left the most difficult issue for the last: do we condemn the terrorist attack as utterly evil regardless of what motivated it, or do we seek refuge in relativism? If it is admitted that one person's terrorist is another person's freedom fighter, how can we avoid the relativist's stance? Mayor Rudolph Giuliani, in his speech to the United Nations, declared that "the era of moral relativism must end" (*The New York Times*, Tuesday, October 2, B5). My own strong inclination is to side with Giuliani, at least regarding September 11, but only if the following tragedies in human history are added to the list: the Holocaust, slavery, refugee camps, the dropping of atomic bombs on Hiroshima and Nagasaki, and possibly the Allied firebombing of Dresden during World War II. I am even inclined to add widespread poverty to this list, and indeed any form of massive and systematic discrimination. In a sense, then, I agree with Edgerton's position, described in Chapter Three, that not everything that happens in human interaction can be considered positive and useful. Where I differ is in thinking that if there is any correlation between so-called civilized societies and human benevolence, it may well be a negative one.

NOTES

1. Possibly like most of us, I had two different reactions to the events of September 11. The first was emotional: the gut-wrenching identification with human suffering. The second was intellectual: what motivated the attack? It would be less than honest if I did not state that had my wife, daughter or son been caught in the World Trade Center or the Pentagon, I too would be crying for retribution rather than playing around with ideas. As it is often remarked, when faced with a crisis, emotion readily triumphs over reason.

It would be equally dishonest, especially in view of my sometimes critical comments below, If I denied being personally comforted by the efforts in progress to make the world a safer place.

2. According to Juergensmeyer (2000), in the last three decades there has been a sharp increase in the number of terrorist groups motivated by religion. For other recent general works on terrorism, see Laqueur (1999) and Stern (2000). For a specific focus on the Taliban in Afghanistan and bin Laden, see Huband (1998), Rashid (2001) and Reeve (1999).

3. The September 11 terrorist attack is one of those triggering factors setting off racism that I describe in my scheme "Conceptualizing Racism" in Chapter Three. Globalization may well qualify as a key dimension in level two of that same scheme—a structural-political dimension of universal and enduring significance.

4. If the anti-globalization protesters thought they were harshly dealt with by government forces in the past, that will resemble a tea party compared to their probable treatment following September 11.

5. Regarding these charges against Israel, my opinion is that if it suddenly found itself at peace with its neighbors, its "excesses" would quickly dissipate. The curtailment of civil liberties, jingoism, and even racial stereotyping are not unique to Israel. They have intruded everywhere among nations at war, and are very much evident in the United States and Canada now.

6. Many years ago, when I was a young man, I hitchhiked across the entire stretch of North Africa, and well remember the repeated statement that the one thing that unites Arabs is their all-consuming hatred for Israel.

7. I cannot help expressing my dismay regarding the reversal of the trend toward equality. If human rationality and knowledge distinguish us from other species, and if progress and "civilization" mean anything, I would have thought that this would translate into the application of politics to enhance the well-being of all human beings. Instead, the opposite seems to be the case.

8. The term *civilization* is not much used in anthropology today because it runs counter to the relativistic assumption that there are no superior societies. Yet it is interesting to remember that what has probably been the most famous definition of culture in the discipline—Tylor's—included the term civilization, even though it is usually omitted in textbooks.

Tylor's full definition is as follows (Gamst and Norbeck 1976:36; original in Tylor 1873): "Culture or Civilization, taken in its wide ethnographic sense, is that complex whole which includes knowledge, belief, art, morals, law, custom, and any other capabilities and habits acquired by man as a member of society."

9. In view of the rapid growth of Islam in sub-Saharan Africa, and the stagnant economies of that part of the world—no longer the dark continent, but the forgotten continent—one cannot help but wonder whether Africa will produce the next generation's international terrorists, especially if one factors in the already volatile North.

Bibliography

Abu-Lughod, Lila. 1990. "The Romance of Resistance: Tracing Transformations of Power through Bedouin Women." *American Ethnologist* 17: 41–55.

———. 1991. "Writing against Culture." In Richard G. Fox, ed. *Recapturing Anthropology*, pp. 137–162. Santa Fe, NM: School of American Research.

———. 1999. "Comments" *Current Anthropology* 40: 13–15.

Ammerman, Nancy T. 1991. "North American Protestant Fundamentalism." In Martin E. Marty and R. Scott Appleby, eds. *Fundamentalism Observed*. Chicago: University of Chicago Press.

Appadurai, Arjun. 1990. "Disjuncture and Difference in the Global Cultural Economy." In Mike Featherstone, ed. *Global Culture*, pp. 295–310. London: Sage Publications.

———. 1991. "Global Ethnoscapes: Notes and Queries for a Transnational Anthropology." In Richard G. Fox, ed. *Recapturing Anthropology*, pp. 191–210. Santa Fe, NM: School of American Research Press.

Arendt, Hannah. 1986. "Communicative Power." In Steven Lukes, ed. *Power*, pp. 59–73. Oxford: Basil Blackwell.

Argyrou, Vassos. 1999. "Sameness and the Ethnological Will to Meaning." *Current Anthropology* 40: S29–S41.

Bachrach, P., and M.S. Baratz. 1962. "Two Faces of Power." *American Political Science Review* 56: 947–952.

———. 1963. "Decisions and Non-decisions: An Analytic Framework." *American Political Science Review* 57: 632–642.

———. 1970. *Power and Poverty: Theory and Practice*. New York: Oxford University Press.

Bailey, F.G. 1969. *Stratagems and Spoils*. Oxford: Blackwell.

———. 1980. "The Exercise of Power in Complex Organizations." Unpublished Paper for Burg Wartenstein Symposium no. 84.

Baker, D. 1978. "Race and Power: Comparative Approaches to the Analysis of Race Relations." *Ethnic and Racial Studies* 1: 316–335.

Barrett, Stanley R. 1977. *The Rise and Fall of an African Utopia*. Waterloo, ON: Wilfred Laurier University Press.

———. 1979. "From Communalism to Capitalism: Two Phases of Social Control in an African Utopia." *Contemporary Crises* 3: 269–289.

———. 1984. *The Rebirth of Anthropological Theory*. Toronto: University of Toronto Press.

———. 1987. *Is God a Racist? The Right Wing in Canada*. Toronto: University of Toronto Press.

———. 1994. *Paradise: Class, Commuters, and Ethnicity in Rural Ontario*. Toronto: University of Toronto Press.

Barrett, Stanley R., Sean Stokholm, and Jeanette Burke. 2001. "The Idea of Power and the Power of Ideas: A Review Essay." *American Anthropologist* 103:468–480.

Bendix, Reinhold. 1953. "Social Stratification and Political Power." In Reinhold Bendix and Seymour Martin Lipset, eds. *Class, Status and Power*, pp. 596–609. Glencoe, IL: The Free Press.

Benedict, Ruth. 1960. *Race: Science and Politics*. New York: Viking Press.

Bennett, John W. 1987. "Anthropology and the Emerging World Order: The Paradigm of Culture in an Age of Interdependence." In K. Moore, ed. *Waymarks*, pp. 43–69. Notre Dame, IN: University of Notre Dame Press.

Black, Max, ed. 1961. *The Social Theories of Talcott Parsons: A Critical Examination*. Englewood Cliffs, NJ: Prentice-Hall.

Black-Michaud, J. 1975. *Cohesive Force: Feud in the Mediterranean and the Middle East*. New York: St. Martin's Press.

Boas, Franz. 1910. "Changes in Bodily Form of Descendants of Immigrants." Washington: Government Printing Office. Senate Document No. 208, 1st Congress, 2nd session.

———. 1940. *Race, Language and Culture*. New York: Macmillan.

———. 1962 (orig. 1928). *Anthropology and Modern Life*. New York: W.W. Norton.

———. 1963 (orig. 1911). *The Mind of Primitive Man*. New York: Collier Books.

Boddy, Janice, and Michael Lambek, eds. 1997. "Culture at the End of the Boasian Century." *Social Analysis* 41(3).

Boehm, Christopher. 1984. *Blood Revenge: The Anthropology of Feuding in Montenegro and Other Tribal Societies*. Lawrence, KS: University Press of Kansas.

Bohannan, P. 1963. *Social Anthropology*. New York: Holt, Rinehart and Winston.

Bourdiec, Iviu. 1996. *Nationalisme Corse*. Bastia, Corse: Editions U Ribombu.

Bradshaw, Alan. 1976. "A Critique of Steven Lukes' 'Power: a Radical View'." *Sociology* 10: 121–127.

Brettel, Caroline B., ed. 1993. *When They Read What We Write: The Politics of Ethnography*. Westport, CT: Bergin and Garvey.

Brightman, Robert A. 1995. "Forget Culture: Replacement, Transcendence, Relexafication." *Cultural Anthropology* 10: 509–546.

Brown, Michael F. 1996. "On Resisting Resistance." *American Anthropologist* 98 (4): 729–735.

Brumann, Christoph. 1998. "The Anthropological Study of Globalization." *Anthropos* 93: 495–506.

———. 1999. "Writing for Culture: Why a Successful Concept Should Not Be Discarded." *Current Anthropology* 40: S1–S27.

Burke, Jeanette. 1999. "Consuming 'Culture'." MA thesis. Department of Sociology and Anthropology, University of Guelph.

Busquet, J. 1920. *Le Droit de la Vendetta et Les Paci Corses*. Paris: A. Pedone, ed.

Champlin, John R. ed. 1971. *Power*. New York: Atherton Press.

Claessen, Heni J.M. 1979. "Introduction." In S. Lee Seaton and H. Claessen, eds. *Political Anthropology*. The Hague: Mouton, pp. 7–28.

Clifford, James. 1983. "On Ethnographic Authority." *Representations* 1:118–146.

———. 1988. *The Predicament of Culture*. Cambridge, MA: Harvard University Press.

Clifford, James, and George E. Marcus, eds. 1986. *Writing Culture*. Berkeley: University of California Press.

Cohen, Ronald. 1978. "Introduction." In Ronald Cohen and Elman R. Service, eds. *Origins of the State: The Anthropology of Political Evolution*. Philadelphia: Institute for the Study of Human Issues, pp. 1–20.

Cohen, Ronald, and John Middleton, eds. 1967. *Comparative Political Systems*. Garden City, NY: The Natural History Press.

Collins, Randall. 1981. "On the Microfoundations of Macrosociology." *American Journal of Sociology* 86: 994–1014.

Cox, O. 1948. *Caste, Class and Race*. Garden City, NY: Doubleday.

Dahl, Robert. 1961. *Who Governs?* New Haven, CT: Yale University Press.

———. 1963. *Modern Political Analysis*. Englewood Cliffs, NJ: Prentice-Hall.

———. 1986. "Power as the Control of Behavior." In Steven Lukes, ed. *Power*, pp. 37–58. Oxford: Basil Blackwell.

D'Andrade, Roy. 1999. "Culture Is Not Everything." In E.L. Cerroni-Long, ed. *Anthropological Theory in North America*, pp. 85–103. Westport, CT: Bergin and Garvey.

Darnell, Regna. 1997. "The Anthropological Concept of Culture at the End of the Boasian Century." In Janice Boddy and Michael Lambek, eds. *Culture at the End of the Boasian Century* (special issue). *Social Analysis* 41(3): 42–54.

Demerath, N.J., and R.A. Peterson, eds. 1967. *System, Change and Conflict*. New York: The Free Press.

Digeser, Peter. 1992. "The Fourth Face of Power." *The Journal of Politics* 54: 977–1007.

Durham, M.E. 1928. *Some Tribal Origins, Laws and Customs of the Balkans*. London: George Allan and Unwin Ltd.

Durkheim, E., and Mauss, M. 1963 (orig. 1903). *Primitive Classification*. London: Cohen and West.

Edgerton, Robert B. 1978. "The Study of Deviance, Marginal Man or Everyman." In G. Spindler, ed. *The Making of Psychological Anthropology*, pp. 444–471. Berkeley: University of California Press.

———. 1999. "Maladaptation: A Challenge to Relativism." In E.L. Cerroni-Long, ed. *Anthropological Theory in North America*, pp. 55–75. Westport, CT: Bergin and Garvey.

Edwards, Harry. 1974. "The Myth of the Racially Superior Athlete." In George H. Gage, ed. *Sport and American Society*, pp. 346–352. Menlo Park, CA: Addison-Wesley.

Eidlin, Fred. Unpublished Manuscript. "The Power and Powerlessness of the Communist Power System." Department of Political Science, University of Guelph.

Eller, Jack David. 1997. "Anti-Anti-Multiculturalism" *American Anthropologist* 99 (2): 249–260.

Emmet, Dorothy. 1971. "The Concept of Power." In John R. Champlin, ed. *Power*, pp. 78–103. New York: Atherton Press.

Etzioni, Amitai. 1993. "Power as a Societal Force." In Marvin E. Olsen and Martin N. Marger, eds. *Power in Modern Societies*, pp. 18–28. Boulder, CO: Westview Press.

Fabian, Johannes. 1991. *Time and the Work of Anthropology: Critical Essays, 1971–1991.* Reading, England: Harwood Academic Publishers.

Featherstone, Mike, ed. 1990. *Global Culture.* London: Sage Publications.

———. 1995. *Undoing Culture: Globalization, Postmodernism and Identity.* London: Sage Publications.

Firth, R. 1956. *Human Types.* New York: Barnes and Noble, Inc.

Fortes, M., and E.E. Evans-Pritchard, eds. 1940. *African Political Systems.* London: Oxford University Press.

Foucault, Michel. 1978. *The History of Sexuality,* Vol. 1. Trans. Robert Hurley. New York: Pantheon Books.

———. 1980. *Power/Knowledge.* Colin Gordon, ed. and trans. Brighton, Sussex: The Harvester Press Ltd.

———. 1982. *Beyond Structuralism and Hermeneutics.* Hubert Dreyfus and Paul Rabinow, eds. Chicago: University of Chicago Press.

———. 1984. *The Foucault Reader.* Paul Rabinow, ed. New York: Pantheon Books.

———. 1988. *Michel Foucault: Politics, Philosophy, Culture.* Lawrence D. Kritzman, ed. New York: Routledge.

Frank, André Gunder. 1966. "The Development of Underdevelopment." *Monthly Review* 18: 17–31.

Freilich, Morris,. ed. 1972. *The Meaning of Culture.* Lexington, MA: Xerox College Publishing.

Fried, Morton H. 1967. *The Evolution of Political Society.* New York: Random House.

———. 1972. *The Study of Anthropology.* New York: Thomas Y. Crowell Company.

Friedman, Jonathan. 1990. "Being in the World: Globalization and Localization." In Mike Featherstone, ed. *Global Culture,* pp. 311–328. London: Sage Publications.

———. 1994. *Cultural Identity and Global Process.* London: Sage Publications.

Galbraith, John Kenneth. 1983. *The Anatomy of Power.* Boston: Houghton Mifflin.

Gamst, F.C., and E. Norbeck, eds. 1976. *Ideas of Culture: Sources and Uses.* New York: Holt, Rinehart and Winston.

Gane, Mike, ed. 1986. *Towards a Critique of Foucault.* London: Routledge and Kegan Paul.

Geertz, Clifford. 1973. *The Interpretation of Cultures.* New York: Basic Books.

———. 1984. "Distinguished Lecture: Anti Anti-Relativism." *American Anthropologist* 86: 263–278.

Gellner, Ernest. 1983. *Nations and Nationalism.* Oxford: Basil Blackwell.

Giddens, A. 1968. "'Power' in the Recent Writings of Talcott Parsons." *Sociology* 2: 257–272.

———. 1979. *Central Problems in Social Theory.* London: Macmillan.

Giudici, Nicolas. 1997. *Le Crépuscule des Corses.* Paris: Bernard Grasset.

Gluckman, Max. 1956. *Custom and Conflict in Africa.* Oxford: Basil Blackwell.

Goodenough, Ward. 1994. "Toward a Working Theory of Culture." In Robert Borofsky, ed. *Assessing Cultural Anthropology,* pp. 262–275. New York: McGraw-Hill.

Goody, Jack. 1994. "Culture and Its Boundaries: A European View." In Robert Borofsky, ed. *Assessing Cultural Anthropology,* pp. 250–261. New York: McGraw-Hill.

Gordon, James. 2001. "Bomb them with Butter." Guelph, Ontario, Canada.

Gruneau, Richard. 1982. "Sport and the Debate on the State." In Hart Cantelon and Richard Gruneau, eds. *Sport, Culture and the Modern State,* pp. 1–38. Toronto: University of Toronto Press.

Gupta, Akhil, and James Ferguson. 1992. "Beyond 'Culture': Space, Identity, and the Politics of Difference." *Cultural Anthropology* 7 (1): 6–23.

Habermas, Jurgen. 1986. "Hannah Arendt's Communications Concept of Power." In Steven Lukes, ed. *Power*, pp. 75–93. Oxford: Basil Blackwell.

Hannerz, Ulf. 1986. "Theory in Anthropology: Small is Beautiful? The Problem of Complex Cultures." *Comparative Studies in Society and History* 28 (2): 362–367.

———. 1989. "Notes on the Global Ecumene." *Public Culture* 1 (2): 66–75.

———. 1990. "Cosmopolitans and Locals in World Culture." In Mike Featherstone, ed. *Global Culture*, pp. 237–251. London: Sage Publications.

———. 1992. *Cultural Complexity*. New York: Columbia University Press.

———. 1997. "Borders." *UNESCO* 49: 537–548.

Hanson, Allan. 1990. "The Making of the Maori: Culture Invention and Its Logic." *American Anthropologist* 91: 890–902.

Hargreaves, John. 1982. "Sport and Hegemony." In Hart Cantelon and Richard Gruneau, eds. *Sport, Culture and the Modern State*, pp. 103–140. Toronto: University of Toronto Press.

Harris, Marvin. 1971. *Culture, Man and Nature*. New York: Thomas Y. Crowell Company.

———. 1975. *Cows, Pigs, Wars and Witches*. New York: Vintage Books.

———. 1979. *Cultural Materialism: The Struggle for a Science of Culture*. New York: Random House.

Hasluck, Margaret. 1954. *The Unwritten Law in Albania*. Cambridge: Cambridge University Press.

Herzfeld, Michael. 1997. "Anthropology and the Problem of Significance." *Social Analysis* 41 (3): 107–138.

Hier, Sean P. 2000. "The Contemporary Structure of Canadian Racial Supremacism: Networks, Strategies and New Technologies." *Canadian Journal of Sociology* 25: 1–24.

Hobbes, Thomas. 1971. "Of Power." In John R. Champlin, ed. *Power*, pp. 69–77. New York: Atherton Press.

Hoberman, John. 1997. *Darwin's Athletes: How Sport Has Damaged Black America and Preserved the Myth of Race*. Boston: Houghton Mifflin.

Hobsbawm, Eric. 1983. "Introduction: Inventing Traditions." In Eric Hobsbawm and Terence Ranger, eds. *The Invention of Tradition*, pp. 1–14. Cambridge: Cambridge University Press.

———. 1990. *Nations and Nationalism Since 1790*. Cambridge: Cambridge University Press.

Horowitz, Irving Louis. 1967. "An Introduction to C. Wright Mills." In Irving Louis Horowitz, ed. *Power, Politics and People: The Collected Essays of C. Wright Mills*, pp. 1–20. New York: Oxford University Press.

Huband, Mark. 1998. *Warriors of the Prophet: The Struggle for Islam*. Boulder, CO: Westview Press.

Hughes, D., and Kallen, E. 1974. *The Anatomy of Racism*. Montreal: Harvest House.

Hunter, Floyd. 1953. *Community Power Structure*. Chapel Hill: The University of North Carolina Press.

Isaac, Jeffrey C. 1987. *Power and Marxist Theory: A Realist View*. Ithaca, NY: Cornell University Press.

Jahoda, M. 1961. "Race Relations and Mental Health." In UNESCO, *Race and Science,* pp. 453–91. New York: Columbia University Press.

Jarvie, I.C. 1983. "Rationalism and Relativism." *The British Journal of Sociology* 34: 44–60.

Juergensmeyer, Mark. 2000. *Terror in the Mind of God: The Global Rise of Religious Violence.* Berkeley: University of California Press.

Kahn, Joel. 1989. "Culture: Demise or Resurrection?" *Critique of Anthropology* 9 (2): 5–25.

Kane, Martin. 1971. "An Assessment of 'Black Is Best'." *Sports Illustrated* 34 (Jan. 18): 73–83.

Kaplan, D., and R. Manners. 1972. *Culture Theory.* Englewood Cliffs, NJ: Prentice-Hall.

Keesing, Roger M. 1976. *Cultural Anthropology.* New York: Holt, Rinehart and Winston.

———. 1994. "Theories of Culture Revisited." In Robert Borofsky, ed. *Assessing Cultural Anthropology,* pp. 301–312. New York: McGraw-Hill.

King, Anthony. 1990. "Architecture, Capital and the Globalization of Culture." In Mike Featherstone, ed. *Global Culture,* pp. 397–411. London: Sage Publications.

Kornhauser, William. 1966. "'Power Elite' or 'Veto Groups'?" In Reinhold Bendix and Seymour Martin Lipset, eds. *Class, Status and Power,* pp. 210–218. Second ed. New York: The Free Press.

Kroeber, A. 1963 (orig. 1923). *Anthropology: Culture Patterns and Processes.* New York: Harcourt, Brace and World.

Kuper, Adam. 1988. *The Invention of Primitive Society: Transformation of an Illusion.* London and New York: Routledge.

Kurtz, Donald V. 1979. "Political Anthropology: Issues and Trends on the Frontier." In |S. Lee Seaton and Heni J.M. Claessen, eds. *Political Anthropology,* pp. 31–62. The Hague: Mouton.

———. 2001. *Political Anthropology: Paradigms and Power.* Boulder, CO: Westview Press.

Laqueur, Walter. 1999. *The New Terrorism: Fanaticism and the Arms of Mass Destruction.* New York: Oxford University Press.

Leach, E.R. 1954. *Political Systems of Highland Burma.* Boston: Beacon Press.

Lenski, G. 1966. *Power and Privilege.* New York: McGraw-Hill.

Lévi-Strauss, Claude. 1974 (orig. 1955). *Tristes Tropiques.* New York: Atheneum.

———. 1994. "Anthropology, Race, and Politics: A Conversation with Didier Eribon." In Robert Borofsky, ed. *Assessing Cultural Anthropology,* pp. 1–21. New York: McGraw-Hill.

Lévy-Bruhl, Lucien. 1985 (orig. 1910). *How Natives Think.* L.A. Clare, trans. Princeton, NJ: Princeton University Press.

Lewis, Herbert S. 1998. "The Misrepresentation of Anthropology and Its Consequences." *American Anthropologist* 100: 716–731.

Lieberman, Leonard. 1997. "Gender and the Deconstruction of the Race Concept." *American Anthropologist* 99 (3): 545–558.

Lieberman, Leonard, et al. 1992. "Race in Biology and Anthropology: A Study of College Texts and Professors." *Journal of Research in Science Teaching* 29 (3):301–321.

Lipset, S., and E. Raab. 1970. *The Politics of Unreason: Right-Wing Extremism in America, 1790–1970.* New York: Harper and Row.

Lloyd, P.C. 1960. "Sacred Kingship and Government among the Yoruba." *Africa* 30: 221–237.

———. 1967. "The Traditional Political System of the Yoruba." In Ronald Cohen and John Middleton, eds. *Comparative Political Systems*, pp. 269–292. Garden City, NY: The Natural History Press.

———. 1968. "Conflict Theory and Yoruba Kingdoms." A.S.A. Monographs 7. *History and Social Anthropology*, pp. 25–61. London: Tavistock Publications.

Lukes, Steven. 1974. *Power: A Radical View*. London: Macmillan.

———. 1976. "Reply to Bradshaw." *Sociology* 10: 129–132.

———. 1977. *Essays in Social Theory*. London: Macmillan.

———. ed. 1986. *Power*. Oxford: Basil Blackwell Ltd.

MacKinnon, Neil J. 1994. *Symbolic Interactionism as Affect Control*. Albany, NY: State University of New York Press.

Malinowski, B. 1941. "An Anthropological Analysis of War." *American Journal of Sociology* XLVI: 521–550.

Mann, Michael. 1993. "The Autonomous Power of the State." In Marvin E. Olsen and Martin N. Marger, eds. *Power in Modern Societies*. Boulder, CO: Westview Press, pp. 314–327.

Marcaggi, J. 1978. *Bandits Corses D'Hier et D'Aujourd'hui*. Ajaccio: Librarie La Marge.

Mascia-Lees, Frances E., et al. 1989. "The Postmodernist Turn in Anthropology: Cautions from a Feminist Perspective." *Signs* 15: 7–33.

Maxwell, Joseph A. 1999. "A Realist/Postmodern Concept of Culture." In E.L. Cerroni-Long, ed. *Anthropological Theory in North America*, pp. 143–173. Westport, CT: Bergin and Garvey.

McClelland, Charles A. 1971. "Power and Influence." In John R. Champlin, ed. *Power*, pp. 35–65. New York: Atherton Press.

McCelland, David C. 1975. *Power: The Inner Experience*. New York: Irvington Publishers, Inc.

McMurtry, John. 1998. *Unequal Freedoms: The Global Market as an Ethical System*. Toronto: Garamond Press.

Merrington, J. 1968. "Theory and Practice in Gramsci's Marxism." *Socialist Register*: 145–176.

Michaels, Walter Benn. 1992. "Race Into Culture." *Critical Inquiry* 18: 655–685.

Middleton, John, and David Tait, eds. 1958. *Tribes Without Rulers*. London: Routledge and Kegan Paul Ltd.

Mills, C. Wright. 1956 (orig. 1951). *White Collar*. New York: Oxford University Press.

———. 1959. *The Sociological Imagination*. New York: Oxford University Press.

———. 1964 (orig. 1956). *The Power Elite*. New York: Oxford University Press.

———. 1967 (orig. 1963). *Power, Politics and People: The Collected Essays of C. Wright Mills*. Louis Horowitz, ed. New York: Oxford University Press.

Montagu, Ashley. 1957. *The Natural Superiority of Women*. New York: The Macmillan Company.

Moodley, K. 1981. "Canadian Ethnicity in Comparative Perspective: Issues in the Literature." In J. Dahlie and T. Fernando, eds. *Ethnicity, Power and Politics in Canada*, pp. 6–21. Toronto: Metheun.

Moore, John H. 1974. "The Culture Concept as Ideology." *American Ethnologist* 1: 537–549.

Moore, Sally Falk. 1994. "The Ethnography of the Present and the Analysis of Process." In Robert Borofsky, ed. *Assessing Cultural Anthropology*, pp. 362–376. New York: McGraw-Hall.

Mukhopadhyay, Carol C., and Yolanda T. Moses. 1997. "Reestablishing 'Race' in An-
    thropological Discourse." *American Anthropologist* 99 (3): 517–531.
Murphy, Robert. 1971. *The Dialectics of Social Life*. New York: Basic Books.
Nash, Manning. 1991. "Islamic Resurgence in Malaysia and Indonesia." In Martin E.
    Marty and R. Scott Appleby, eds. *Fundamentalism Observed*. Chicago: Univer-
    sity of Chicago Press.
Needham, R. 1979. *Symbolic Classification*. Santa Monica, CA: Goodyear Publishing.
Nicholas, Ralph W. 1965. "Factions: a Comparative Analysis." In M. Banton, ed. *Political
    Systems and the Distribution of Power*. London: Tavistock Publications, pp. 21–62.
———. 1976. "Segmentary Factional Political systems. In Marc J. Swartz et al., eds. *Po-
    litical Anthropology*, pp. 49–59. Chicago: Aldine Publishing Company.
Olsen, Marvin E., and Martin N. Marger, eds. 1993. *Power in Modern Societies*. Boulder,
    CO: Westview Press.
Omi, Michael, and Howard Winant. 1986. *Racial Formation in the United States from
    the 1960s to the 1980s*. New York and London: Routledge.
Ortner, Sherry B. 1991. "Reading America: Preliminary Notes on Class and Culture." In
    Richard G. Fox, ed. *Recapturing Anthropology*, pp. 163–189. Santa Fe, NM: School
    of American Research Press.
———. 1995. "Resistance and the Problem of Ethnographic Refusal." *Comparative Stud-
    ies in Society and History* 37 (1): 173–193.
Parkin, David. 1990. "Eastern Africa: The View from the Office and the Voice from the
    Field." In Richard Fardon, ed. *Localizing Strategies: Regional Traditions of Ethno-
    graphic Writing*, pp. 182–203. Edinburgh: Scottish Academic Press.
Parsons, Talcott. 1951. *The Social System*. Glencoe, IL: The Free Press.
———. 1960. *Structure and Process in Modern Societies*. New York: The Free Press.
———. 1964. *Essays in Sociological Theory*. Revised. Glencoe, IL: The Free Press.
———. 1966. "On the Concept of Political Power." In R. Bendix and S.M. Lipset, eds.
    Class, Status and Power. Second ed., pp. 210–218. New York: The Free Press.
Peter, K. 1981. "The Myth of Multiculturalism and Other Political Fables." In J. Dahlie
    and T. Fernando, eds. *Ethnicity, Power and Politics in Canada*, pp. 56–67. Toronto:
    Metheun.
Peters, E. 1967. "Some Structural Aspects of the Feud among the Camel-Herding Bedouin
    of Cyrenaica." *Africa* 37: 261–282.
Pomponi, F. 1979. *Histoire de la Corse*. Hachette.
Prager, J. 1972. "White Racial Privilege and Social Change: An Examination of Theories
    of Racism." *Berkeley Journal of Sociology* 17: 117–150.
Rabinow, Paul. 1986. "Representations Are Social Facts: Modernity and Post-Modernity
    in Anthropology." In James Clifford and George E. Marcus, eds. *Writing Culture*,
    pp. 234–261. Berkeley, CA: University of California Press.
Rashid, Ahmed. 2001. *Taliban: Militant Islam, Oil and Fundamentalism in Central Asia*.
    New Haven, CT: Yale University Press.
Reeve, Simon. 1999. *The New Jackals: Ramzi Yousef, Osama bin Laden and the Future
    of Terrorism*. Evanston, IL: Northwestern University Press.
Reisman, David. 1956. *The Lonely Crowd*. Garden City, NY: Doubleday.
Rex, J. 1970. *Race Relations in Sociological Theory*. New York: Schocken Books.
Robbins, R. 1999. *Global Problems and the Culture of Capitalism*. Boston: Allyn and
    Bacon.

Rosaldo, Renato. 1994. "Whose Cultural Studies?" *American Anthropologist* 96: 525–529.

Rose, A. 1971. "Antisemitism's Root in City Hatred." In L. Dinnerstein, ed. *Antisemitism in the United States*, pp. 41–47. New York: Holt, Rinehart and Winston.

Ruane, Joseph, and Jennifer Todd. 1991. "Why Can't You Get Along with Each Other? Culture, Structure and the Northern Ireland Conflict." In Eamonn Hughes, ed. *Culture and Politics in Northern Ireland 1960–1990*. Milton Keynes: Open University Press, pp. 27–43.

Russell, Bertrand. 1938. *Power: A New Social Analysis*. New York: W.W. Norton.

Said, Edward W. 1979. *Orientalism*. New York: Vintage Books.

Sangren, P. Steven. 1988. "Rhetoric and the Authority of Ethnography." *Current Anthropology* 29: 405–424.

———. 1995. "'Power' against Ideology: A Critique of Foucaultian Usage." *Cultural Anthropology* 10 (1): 3–40.

Scheper-Hughes, Nancy. 1982. *Saints, Scholars and Schizophrenics*. Berkeley: University of California Press.

Schwarzweller, H. 1979. "Migration and the Changing Rural Scene." *Rural Sociology* 44: 7–23.

Scott, James C. 1985. *Weapons of the Weak: Everyday Forms of Peasant Resistance*. New Haven: Yale University Press.

Selsam, H. et al., eds. 1970. *Dynamics of Social Change: A Reader in Marxist Social Science*. New York: International Publishers.

Service, E.R. 1975. *Origins of the State and Civilization: The Process of Cultural Evolution*. New York: W.W. Norton.

Shanklin, Eugenia. 1998. "The Profession of the Color-Blind: Sociocultural Anthropology and Racism in the 21st Century." *American Anthropologist* 100: 669–679.

Simeoni, Edmond. 1975. *Le Piege d'Aleria*. Paris: J. Clattès.

Singer, Merrill. 1993. "Knowledge for Use: Anthropology and Community-Centered Substance Abuse Research." *Social Science Medicine*. 37: 15–25.

Smith, Anthony D. 1990. "Towards a Global Culture?" In Mike Featherstone, ed. *Global Culture*, pp. 171–191. London: Sage Publications.

Smith, M.G. 1966. "Pre-Industrial Stratification Systems." In N.J. Smelser and S.M. Lipset, eds. *Social Structure and Mobility in Economic Development*, pp. 141–176. Chicago: Aldine Publishing.

Spinrad, William. 1966. "Power in Local Communities." In Reinhold Bendix and Seymour Martin Lipset, eds. *Class, Status and Power*, pp. 218–231. Second ed. New York: The Free Press.

Stember, C.H. 1976. *Sexual Racism*. New York: Elsevier.

Stern, Jessica. 2000. *The Ultimate Terrorist*. Boston, MA: Harvard University Press.

Steward, Julian. 1955. *Theory of Culture Change*. Urbana: University of Illinois Press.

Swartz, Marc J. ed. 1968. *Local-Level Politics*. Chicago: Aldine Publishing Company.

Swartz, Marc J. et al., eds. 1976. *Political Anthropology*. Chicago: Aldine Publishing Company.

Tiffany, Walter W. 1979. "New Directions in Political Anthropology." In S. Lee Seaton and Heni J.M. Claessen, eds. *Political Anthropology*, pp. 63–75. The Hague: Mouton.

Trouillot, Michel-Rolph. 1991. "Anthropology and the Savage Slot: The Poetics and Politics of Otherness." In Richard G. Fox, ed. *Recapturing Anthropology*, pp. 17–44. Santa Fe, NM: School of American Research Press.

Turner, Terence, 1993. "Anthropology and Multiculturalism." *Cultural Anthropology* 8: 411–429.

Tylor, Edward B. 1976. "The Science of Culture." In Frederick C. Gamst and Edward Norbeck, eds., *Ideas of Culture*, pp. 36–43. New York: Holt, Rinehart and Winston.

———. 1873. *Primitive Culture*. John Murray (Publishers) Ltd.

Vayda, Andrew P. 1994. "Actions, Variations, and Change: The Emerging Anti-Essentialist View in Anthropology." In Robert Borofsky, ed. *Assessing Cultural Anthropology*, pp. 320–328. New York: McGraw-Hill.

Verdon, Michel. 1998. *Rethinking Households*. London and New York: Routledge.

Vidich, A., and J. Bensman. 1958. *Small Town in Mass Society*. Princeton: Princeton University Press.

Visweswaran, Kamala. 1998. "Race and the Culture of Anthropology." *American Anthropologist* 100 (1): 70–83.

Wallace, Anthony F.C. 1970. *Culture and Personality*. New York: Random House.

Wallace, Max. 1988. "NHL Has Long History of Racism." *The Fulcrum*. Dec. 1 (p. 23) and Dec. 8 (p.13).

Wallerstein, Immanuel. 1974. *The Modern World-System*. New York: Academic Press.

Weber, Max. 1947 (reprinted 1964). *The Theory of Social and Economic Organization*. T. Parsons and A.M. Henderson, trans. New York: The Free Press.

———. 1949. Edward A. Shils and Henry A. Finch, eds. and trans. *The Methodology of the Social Sciences*. New York: The Free Press.

———. 1958. *The Protestant Ethic and the Spirit of Capitalism*. Talcott Parsons, trans. New York: Charles Scribner's Sons.

———. 1971 (orig. 1922). *The Sociology of Religion*. Ephraim Fischoff, trans., Introduction by Talcott Parsons. Social Science Paperback. London: Methuen.

Weinberg, Ian. 1969. "The Problems of Convergence of Industrial Societies: A Critical Look at the State of a Theory." *Comparative Studies in Society and History* 1: 1–15.

Weissleder, Wolfgang. 1978. "Aristotle's Concept of Political Structure and the State." In Ronald Cohen and Elman R. Service, eds. *Origins of the State: The Anthropology of Political Evolution*, pp. 187–203. Philadelphia: Institute for the Study of Human Issues.

"What Ever Happened to the White Athlete?" 1997. *Sports Illustrated* 87 (Dec. 8): 30–55.

White, Leslie A. 1976. "The Concept of Culture." In F.C. Gamst and E. Norbeck, eds. *Ideas of Culture: Sources and Uses*, pp. 55–71. New York: Holt, Rinehart and Winston.

Whittaker, Elvi. 1992. "Culture: The Reification Under Seige." *Studies in Symbolic Interaction* 13 (107–117).

Wickham, Gary. 1986. "Power and Power Analysis: Beyond Foucault?" In Mike Gane, ed. *Towards a Critique of Foucault*, pp. 149–179. London: Routledge and Kegan Paul.

Willis, W.S. 1969. "Skeletons in the Anthropological Closet." In Dell Hymes, ed. *Reinventing Anthropology*, pp. 121–152. New York: Pantheon Books.

Wilson, Stephen. 1988. *Feuding, Conflict and Banditry in Nineteenth-Century Corsica*. Cambridge: University of Cambridge Press.

Winter, D.G. 1973. *The Power Motive*. New York: The Free Press.

Wolf, Eric. 1966. *Peasants*. Englewood Cliffs, NJ: Prentice-Hall, Inc.

———. 1969. *Peasant Wars of the Twentieth Century*. New York: Harper and Row, Publishers.

————. 1982. *Europe and the People without History*. Berkeley and Los Angeles: University of California Press.

————. 1994. "Perilous Ideas: Race, Culture, People." *Current Anthropology* 35 (1): 1–7.

————. 1999. *Envisioning Power: Ideologies of Dominance and Crisis*. Berkeley: University of California Press.

Worsley, Peter. 1970. *The Trumpet Shall Sound*. St. Albans, England: Paladin.

Wrong, Dennis H. 1979. *Power: Its Forms, Bases and Uses*. Oxford: Basil Blackwell.

Yengoyan, Aram A. 1986. "Theory in Anthropology: On the Demise of the Concept of Culture." *Comparative Studies in Society and History* 28 (2): 368–374.

Index

Abu-Lughod, Lila, 5, 7, 39; on culture, 45, 49; on resistance, 40
Acephalous societies, 22
Action, knowledge and, 70–71
Administration, Smith on, 23
Afghanistan, Taliban and, 117
Africa: indigenous states, 21–22; Islam in, 128 n.9. *See also* West Africa
African Americans, September 11, 2001, and, 127
African-origin people, in sports, 60
African Political Systems (Fortes and Evans-Pritchard), 21, 22, 25
Agency, 110; vs. structure, 27
Albania, vendetta in, 96
Al Qaeda, 119
Ambition, degrees of, 30–31
America: fundamentalism in, 126
America, Muslim perspective on, 125
Americanization, global cultural uniformity as, 11
Ammerman, Nancy T., 126
Anger tactic, 29–30
Anthropologists, on stratification, 55–56
Anthropology: crisis in, 8–10; and imperialism, 7; invented, 47; political, 21; study of race in, 56–57

Anti-autonomous, anti-independence movement, in Corsica, 100
Anti-Catholicism, in Ontario village, 106
Anti-essentialist view, of culture, 48
Anti-globalization protesters, 128 n.4
Anti-racism, Klan and, 92
Anti-relativists, on knowledge and power, 70
Anti-Semitism: in Canada, 88–94; in Hitler's Germany, 52; social change and, 124
Aphrodisiac, power as, 74
Appadurai, Arjun, 5, 6, 11
Arabs. *See* Islam
Arab world, September 11, 2001, attacks and, 121–22
Arcand, Adrien, 88
Arendt, Hannah, 34; force, power, and, 67, 125; resistance, power, and, 73
Argyrou, Vassos, 4
Aryan Nations, 90
Asad, 23–24
"Assessment of 'Black Is Best,' An", 60
Asymmetry of power, 71
Athleticism, of African-origin people, 60

About the Author

STANLEY R. BARRETT is Professor of Anthropology, University of Guelph, Ontario.